# PITFALLS IN PREACHING

# PITFALLS
# *in* PREACHING

Richard L. Eslinger

WILLIAM B. EERDMANS PUBLISHING COMPANY
GRAND RAPIDS, MICHIGAN / CAMBRIDGE, U.K.

© 1996 Wm. B. Eerdmans Publishing Co.
255 Jefferson Ave. S.E., Grand Rapids, Michigan 49503
All rights reserved

Printed in the United States of America

01 00 99 98 97 96    7 6 5 4 3 2 1

**Library of Congress Cataloging-in-Publication Data**

Eslinger, Richard L. (Richard Laurence), 1940-    .
    Pitfalls in preaching / Richard L. Eslinger.
        p.    cm.
    Includes bibliographical references.
    ISBN 0-8028-0820-4 (pbk.: alk. paper)
    1. Preaching.   2. Bible — Homiletical use.   I. Title.
BV4221.E75  1996
251 — dc20                        96-20843
                            CIP

# Contents

CONTENTS

*For Elise,*
*covenant partner;*
*pathway through my pitfalls.*

# Acknowledgments

The first acknowledgment I need to make in a book on preaching's pitfalls is to the United Methodist congregations I have served: in downtown Boston, in a university church in Seattle, in rural southern Indiana, and now here in "Michiana" near South Bend, Indiana. Like every other preacher, I have fallen into homiletical pitfalls in every one of my churches, and my hearers have responded with grace and with helpful instruction. I am also grateful for the colleagues in the ministry of preaching who have attended my workshops on preaching around the country, both within the United Methodist Church and ecumenically. I have learned much from these brothers and sisters. It is a sign of the ecumenical scene today that my research for *Pitfalls in Preaching* was accomplished chiefly at two fine Catholic libraries — at Saint Meinrad School of Theology in southern Indiana and at the University of Notre Dame in South Bend. Moreover, I am deeply indebted to my students in preaching at the Institute of Pastoral Studies at Loyola University at Chicago, who were the first to review and respond to this manuscript.

Several persons must be named out of the many whose imprint is on this book on preaching. First, I wish to thank Dean Rebecca Chopp of Chandler Theological School in Atlanta and Professor James F. White of the University of Notre Dame for permitting me to make reference to them in the pitfall on "Term Papers and Slide Shows." Craig Noll is the editor at Eerdmans who carefully transformed this writer's pitfall-filled manuscript into a readable book,

## ACKNOWLEDGMENTS

and Jennifer Hoffman saw the book through its final stages to completion. Finally, my wife, Elise, has both supported this project with persistence and remained a constant source of encouragement. She is a covenant partner who shares a pathway with me through all the pitfalls. I dedicate this book to her.

# Introduction

This book is a sign of the times for preaching. It is one indication that what we may call the new homiletics has emerged, and in fact has been with us for a while now. It has been advocated by a variety of postmodern homileticians and analyzed as to its methodologies and approaches to Scripture; indeed, it has governed how a good many of us have preached for several years now. In common with the development of other new movements in church and society, the first stages of the new homiletics were marked by polemics, by sharp debates about the superiority of the new approach over against the old. According to the old orthodoxy, preaching was to be largely topical and discursive; it comprised a set of approaches to interpretation and method now satirized as "three points and a poem."

The "shock troops" who overran the positions of topical preaching were mainly the preaching-as-storytelling advocates of the 1970s. They attacked the old homiletics for its loss of biblical narrative (it typically treated a biblical story as disposable once its "theme" or "main idea" was extracted) and for its juxtaposition of inappropriate rationalism and excessive emotionalism. Real human experience was lived somewhere in between these poles in regions bypassed by rationalistic points and propositions on the one hand and syrupy anecdotes on the other. The storytellers called for a recovery of the biblical narrative as essential to faithful preaching of the Word; they also insisted on a recovery of the stories of the real people of the community of faith as integral to this biblical preaching. Their motto became "Preaching the Story and Our Stories."

During the 1980s we saw a further maturing of the new homiletics in the publication of a variety of resources based on theological positions that were also contending with each other and especially with the still-dominant old liberalism. We began to see articles and books advocating "preaching as. . . ." In addition to the now-familiar preaching as storytelling, we could read about preaching as liberation theology, as narrative, as metaphor, as feminism, as induction, as phenomenology, as liturgy, and on and on. Since the late 1980s the first fully developed statements of the new homiletics have appeared, containing models of biblical interpretation as well as giving attention to contemporary rhetoric, methodology, and a theology of proclamation. The two "elders" in the tribe of new homileticians are clearly Fred Craddock and David Buttrick.[1] Others also developed comprehensive summaries of preaching in the new context, and still others have surveyed the methodological terrain of the new homiletics.[2]

Two other developments were critical in the rise of this new homiletics and the corresponding decline in the status of topical preaching. First, this period witnessed a bold new approach to the interpretation of the Bible that was supplanting (or at least supplementing) the historical-critical method. Mainly through the insights of literary criticism, a striking and invigorating new way of seeing the parables was offered by biblical scholars, followed by refreshing applications of the method with regard to narrative in the Hebrew Bible and, initially, the Gospels of Mark and John. Soon the church began to see homiletic works drawing on this literary-critical approach to the interpretation of Scripture, along with in-

---

1. See David Buttrick, *Homiletic: Moves and Structures* (Philadelphia: Fortress Press, 1987). For a list of Fred Craddock's publications, see *Listening to the Word: Studies in Honor of Fred B. Craddock,* ed. Gail R. O'Day and Thomas G. Long (Nashville: Abingdon Press, 1993), pp. 7–8. Most of my references to David Buttrick relate to his pioneering studies in postmodern rhetoric (which focuses on how oral language functions in a communal context) and to his analysis of the dynamics of illustration. If I fail to cite his works explicitly, it is only because I have adopted his insights so thoroughly as my own.

2. See, for example, Thomas G. Long, *The Witness of Preaching* (Louisville, Ky.: Westminster/John Knox Press, 1989); Richard Eslinger, *A New Hearing: Living Options in Homiletic Method* (Nashville: Abingdon Press, 1987).

sights from reader-response, structuralist, and various liberationist readings. We were suddenly in a new world of biblical interpretation that was displacing an older one emphasizing rationalism and a romantic notion of inspiration. These developments illustrate the truth that emerging political, social, and theological movements do not suddenly appear out of nowhere. To be sure, a new paradigm often may be said to be aborning when there is a growing sense of unease with the old, even though the way forward may not yet be apparent. Such a sense of unease well characterized the homiletic condition of many of us who preached through the decades of the sixties and seventies. Since we are wedded to the work of biblical interpreters, the new homiletics required the prior development of new fields of biblical studies.[3]

The second dominant factor in the emergence of the new homiletics has been the wonderful surprise of the three-year ecumenical lectionary and the reforms of worship of which it has been a part. A vast sea change has occurred in the way that the Scriptures are read and heard within local churches that are part of the North American ecumenical scene. Many American Christians now hear three lessons read each Lord's Day, coming from the mouths of laymen and laywomen as well as clergy. The sweep of this three-year series allows these same American Christians to hear vastly more of the biblical witness than was heard in the past. That this profound reform in the service of the Word had its origins in the work of the Second Vatican Council must be considered one of the ironies of the faith attributable only to the work of the Spirit. It is frequently pointed out that the advent of the three-year lectionary is one of the central factors behind the present renewal of preaching. The discipline of preaching the lectionary is in turn having a formative effect on the church's theological reflection and the practice of Christian faith.

A book such as this can appear only after a fair amount of preaching has occurred in local churches in terms of the new models. It takes time to spot what works and what doesn't with reference to sermon method. It also takes time to experience the changes in culture and language that will be reflected in altered rhetorical

---

3. On this topic, see Eugene Lowry's excellent article "The Revolution of Sermon Shape," in *Listening to the Word*, pp. 93–112.

usage. It takes time for us to discover how to use the various approaches of the new homiletics and how to wean ourselves from thinking in terms of points, propositions, and main ideas.

Furthermore, the preaching has occurred not in isolation but within communities of faith where persons have gathered to hear the Word read and proclaimed, to pray, and to break bread. The usually unspoken element in the reforms of preaching, then, is the patience and generosity of our hearers in the pews who have borne with us during this era of profound change. They are the ones who have experienced all of the pitfalls of our preaching, doing so usually — and thankfully! — with a grace-filled patience. It is to these faithful ones, and to the Word, that we seek the most faithful pathways in order to proclaim that Word, all the while trying to avoid the numerous pitfalls in preaching.

As I have reflected on these recent developments in homiletics, I have wanted to find a format for presenting some of the obstacles along the path toward a renewed, transformed biblical preaching. What has emerged is a kind of "spotter's guide," laid out in the following sequence:

Rhetoric. We will first explore significant changes in the workings of the specific language of our calling — oral communication within a community — for pitfalls and pathways.

Scripture and Interpretation. Next, we will turn to the perennial challenge of preaching, which involves matters related to the interpretation of Scripture. Many of the interpretative pitfalls here, we will find, are leftover remnants of the old rationalistic preaching that has been the dominant model of the last several generations.

Method. Sermon method is the next arena within which we conduct our search for homiletic pitfalls. It is a fertile field for problems just now as one set of methodological assumptions is being displaced by others newly emerging on the scene or recovered from the tradition.

Illustration. The next likely context for our pitfall spotting is that of illustration. A great number of preaching problems relate to the necessary work of illustration. But watch! Even the way in which we understand the notion of an illustration is shifting within the new homiletics.

**Context and delivery.** Last, we will turn to the usual context for preaching — the community gathered for worship on the Lord's Day. Also, we will explore some pitfalls related to delivery, or more broadly, the issues related through the unspoken communication occurring between preacher and congregation. And just as trains look odd these days without a caboose to signal "The End," this book would be incomplete without the inclusion of a brief postscript as a kind of homiletical caboose. But this note to my readers: *Pitfalls in Preaching* is not designed for the necessity of a front to back cover reading. Begin wherever you like and explore other pitfalls later. You may get entirely sidetracked for a while by the "For further reading" references. In that case, my intended method for this book is most fulfilled!

One final note to the reader. Writing a book on the pitfalls of preaching could be attempted from some ivory tower where the author infrequently preached and mostly reflected on the preaching of others. Such a project would be a failure. Rather, it is as a colleague who also preaches week in and week out in the midst of pastoral ministry that I have noticed and collected these pitfalls and suggest strategies for avoiding them. I cannot hide the fact that many of these pitfalls are here primarily because I discovered them in the course of my own preaching, with the help of my hearers and my homiletic colleagues. The pitfall image comes from the Psalms, which also contains the more positive image of a pathway. My purpose, then, in identifying these pitfalls is that we may journey more faithfully along the pathways to the Word and to God's people in our preaching.

# 1. The Rhetoric of Preaching

Rhetoric is the study of oral communication in a communal context. Each of the elements in this definition is noteworthy. Rhetoric deals with *oral* communication, which is a different genre from writing, from the print medium. And it is interested in how this speech functions in a *communal* context. Language acts in remarkably different ways in one-on-one or small group contexts and within a larger group of persons. Rhetoric is interested specifically in the context of larger groups. Preaching within communities of faith — church and synagogue — may well be the primary phenomenon available for contemporary rhetoric to study. Conversely, those called to preach are keenly interested in how a culture's language functions. After all, faith comes from hearing.

The rhetorical situation today is different from that of our immediate predecessors. We preach in a time when public language has undergone profound shifts. A vast amount of vocabulary only recently present in the vernacular has suddenly dropped out of usage (largely discursive, conceptual terms). In its place, the new technologies, sciences, and social movements have infused the language with different terminologies along with constantly changing jargon. Gender and ethnic references are in flux as well. In fact, it is not an exaggeration to say that the current rhetorical situation is different from that of any who have preached the Gospel before us. We will want to know how this emerging public language is functioning in order to be faithful servants of the Word, for that

Word can be uttered in this new communal speech as well as, if not better than, in the old. Again, Paul's words "faith comes from hearing" provide the incentive to look carefully for any pitfalls in our own rhetoric.

## 1.1. Talking About/Speaking Of

*Conversion to Christian faith means conversion
from one set of images to another.*

Barbara Brown Taylor, "Preaching the Body"

Imagine that you have signed up for a preaching workshop. You find yourself part of a congenial gathering of ecumenical colleagues, which soon gets down to business. Working on a sample sermon based on a lectionary text, the group agrees that urban homelessness is an apt illustration of one portion of Scripture. The workshop leader asks, "How shall we image homelessness in the sermon?" The replies come quickly from the group — "the fear of violence," "hunger," "alienation from institutions and authority," "exposure to the elements" — and the list builds. As you continue, however, you begin to notice a certain colorlessness of the items; you're "talking about" homelessness all right, but you realize that the collective lack of sharp imagery and urgency in your words shows that the group is not really "speaking of" something that touches them very deeply.

You have actually become aware, in fact, of another pitfall in preaching, perhaps one of the most common and pernicious today. This pitfall is simply the failure to use language that is brightly imaged and shaped with a sense of immediacy. Lacking such language, congregations simply tune out the preacher's words; the intended message slips unnoticed from their awareness.

All too often, our preaching employs a kind of speech ("talk about") that, predictably so, is extremely difficult to be heard and retained. Such speech simply cannot form in congregational consciousness. Preaching from within this homiletic pit of "talk about"

2

results in sermons that largely cannot be retained by the hearers. (Estimates of retention are as low as 25 percent of the language spoken.)

Escaping from this rhetorical pitfall will involve a number of shifts in our language of preaching, which will be addressed in this chapter. If we recall that we address not individuals as individuals but persons within a communal context (just as do most biblical texts), then three corrective steps are critical.

## 1. Shift Pronouns

"Talking about" language uses third-person pronouns, which typically convey a sense of distance. In describing the homeless and their despair, we might intone, "They have little hope of getting out of their dilemma; they no longer look to anyone for real intervention."

We can easily shift our address to the second person, however, which helps to bring us over to a "speaking of" mode. "So look, if you're homeless, you soon give up going down to the welfare office, parked in those same lines every day, . . . getting the stares from people at the bus stop as you go in, . . . you just stop looking for help." The pronouns here are communal, as in the southern "y'all."

## 2. Clarify Perspective

Along with switching pronouns away from the third person, we need to clarify the perspective we take toward our subject (see also sec. 4.9 below). For example, in using "we" in our sermon about the homeless, we can speak *from* the perspective of the homeless themselves, or we can adopt a perspective *toward* the homeless (the officials behind the welfare office counter, those who watch from the bus stop, or perhaps those who watch through a window from inside a bus).

Preaching addresses a communal consciousness and uses communal language. "Speaking of" in preaching will locate the hearers

3

in relation to us by using "we" and "you" in forming ideas and experiences. It will then focus this relation by adopting a consistent perspective toward the subject matter of our sermon.

### 3. Kill Enumeration

We preachers must face squarely the fact that "sentences beginning with enumeration will delete from consciousness" (Buttrick, *Homiletic*, p. 212). Enumeration is part of the bygone homiletic model of argumentation, which, as Eugene Lowry observes, is a spatial rather than a temporal model of preaching (see his *Doing Time in the Pulpit*, pp. 11–28).

Now you, the reader, may notice that this "kill enumeration" dictum is in fact item no. 3 in a list, apparently a casualty of its own decree! In response, however, let me remind you that literary language, with its visual character, works quite differently from preaching, with its oral and aural modality. With a printed page in front of them, readers may scan back and forth among the points enumerated. Hearers of sermons, however, do not have this luxury. The numbering and the meanings that are enumerated in their hearing separate from each other rather than fuse in their consciousness. For the congregation, the result is a serious pitfall — ambiguity rather than clarity.

### For further reading

Look at the section "Language" in David Buttrick's *Homiletic* (Philadelphia: Fortress Press, 1987), pp. 173–221. An excellent article on language in preaching is Barbara Brown Taylor's "Preaching the Body," in *Listening to the Word*, ed. Gail R. O'Day and Thomas G. Long (Nashville: Abingdon Press, 1993), pp. 207–21. Also check out Eugene Lowry's distinction between "doing space" and "doing time" in his *Doing Time in the Pulpit: The Relationship between Narrative and Preaching* (Nashville: Abingdon Press, 1985). For an analysis of the method of both Buttrick and Lowry, see chapters 3 and 5 in my *A New Hearing* (Nashville: Abingdon Press, 1987).

## 1.2. We Can't Hear You

Imagine hearing a sermon that begins with the statement, "No man, whenever in history, has lived without the experience of hope." Ignoring for now any content there may be in this proposition, what is wrong rhetorically? Why will this sentence simply delete from congregational consciousness as soon as the words have been uttered?

Perhaps the first thing we notice is the sexist usage of "man," meaning "all persons." Substituting "person" for "man," however, doesn't gain much for us here. The root problem of this sermon opener is its dependence on conceptual terms of a rather expansive and generic sort. "Man" (or "persons"), "history," and "experience" together are simply too vast and fuzzy in their conceptual character to refer to anything memorable that the congregation might grab on to. Lacking such reference, the sentence will not be retained. (An additional factor here is the fact that first sentences in an oral discourse rarely are retained well by the audience. For the first sentence to be purely abstract and conceptual, as this one is, more than ever guarantees that the congregation will not retain it within their consciousness.)

The pitfall here is that of depending on largely conceptual language to carry meaning within our preaching. The list of such words can easily be expanded and would include theological terms such as "expiation," "atonement," and "eschatology," as well as jargon words, including those ending in "-ize," "-ism," and "-ness" (e.g., "marginalize," "ageism," "brokenness"). In addition, our culture has dropped from the vernacular a huge amount of social vocabulary, consisting especially of broad, generic conceptual terms (e.g., "chivalry," "obeisance," "wherewithal"). To attempt recovery of these fine terms now no longer in the active vocabulary, as one seminary professor has urged, would not result in their recovery as vernacular. Rather, to use these slightly anachronistic words in our preaching would yield sermons having "an odd essayistic tone and be difficult for congregations to grasp" (Buttrick, *Homiletic*, p. 188).

In our time, oral communication within a communal context has increasingly shifted in its store of discourse toward images, metaphors, and stories. In order to avoid the "we can't hear you"

5

pitfall, we need to use primarily the five thousand or so words that compose the social vernacular of our hearers. Interestingly, the vocabulary of Koine Greek in the New Testament includes just about the same number of words, mostly borrowed from then available, public usage.

*Hints:* Teach a youth class in your church school for a term. You don't need to adopt the ever-changing "in" jargon of the youth culture, but notice carefully the social language of the class. It will provide the core vernacular for your preaching.

Notice the language of the latest pronouncements from denominational headquarters. Unfortunately, this is generally language to avoid in your preaching!

In preaching, you can sneak in a theological term now and then if you adopt a strategy of "funning" the language. We might say, for example, "Now the theologians talk about 'eschatology' . . . doesn't that sound nice? — 'eschatology.' But really what they mean is what happens 'when the roll is called up yonder.'"

*For further reading*

Buttrick, David. *Homiletic: Moves and Structures,* pp. 173–98. Philadelphia: Fortress Press, 1987.

Craddock, Fred B. *Preaching,* pp. 196–209. Nashville: Abingdon Press, 1985.

## 1.3. Multimedia, Pyrotechnic, Brain-Boggling Prose

*First, less is more.*

Eugene Lowry, *How to Preach a Parable*

Over the span of television's four and a half decades of influence on our culture and language, visual imagery has exploded into our communal consciousness. The "vocabulary of imagery" continues to proliferate, at a seemingly accelerating rate. Moreover, we have been trained to absorb these images at an ever-quickening pace.

With the sound on your TV turned off, scrutinize an evening's worth of commercials, stopwatch in hand. You will notice that whether the spot is selling a soft drink or a new car, the variety and duration of images presented in the few seconds of the commercial are the same. The videos accompanying popular music on MTV present the same skein of imagery. The amazing diversity of images presented is far more wide-ranging than what one might expect to accompany a mere soft drink or an automobile or a song. This mind-stretching diversity is held together by some unifying theme or mood (in a commercial, say, by the variety of recreational activities of really "with it" baby boomers). Still, the crafters of these visual ads and videos seem to be constantly pushing the limits of the imagery associated with their products and productions.

The other limit being tested concerns the duration of each visual image, with a clear trend toward shorter and shorter exposure times. In present-day cola or auto ads, it is rather unusual for an image to appear on the screen for as "long" as two full seconds. It seems that our visual culture is increasingly capable of assimilating images that are given briefer and briefer periods of exposure. Some commercials even deliberately exceed any person's ability to receive and recall the pastiche of images presented. Here, the goal seems to be to convey an accumulated or layered effect, creating an attitude toward the product that is a construct of these images and image fragments. To judge from the amount of money spent to create and air these imagery overdose commercials, they must be having an amazing effect on our buying patterns!

With these developments in mind, consider some of the recent trends in preaching. Preaching in contemporary North American culture is increasingly visual in its imagery and imagistic in its content. The various approaches representing the new homiletics emphasize the role of the image in the language of preaching. (In fact, one of the hermeneutic issues of this new day in preaching is the cost of translating an *oral* text of biblical narrative into a *visual* presentation of sermonic imagery.) Under the impact of the visual media in general — and, it seems, TV commercials in particular — some preachers have fallen into the pitfall of adopting a kind of pulpit language that resembles the soft drink or automobile ads. Images come tumbling out, diverse, seemingly unarranged, far too many for the hearers to process or recall.

What is happening here? Although we are well beyond the old discursive preaching, with its argumentation and persuasion, its outlines and three points, we still need to be aware of a pitfall unique to our multimedia age. Eugene Lowry offers a useful caution to preachers in this new and mostly uncharted homiletic world: "Those who cram the story line full of obvious metaphors lose the punch because *(a)* listeners cannot handle the mental gymnastics involved in too many metaphoric allusions, and *(b)* once listeners begin to take explicit note of the preacher's overuse of the technique, they distance themselves from its effect" (*How to Preach a Parable,* p. 63).

The multimedia, pyrotechnic, brain-boggling prose that we are hearing in some preaching goes well beyond the scope of more recent approaches that speak of the sermon's "plot" assembled in communal hearing through a sequence of "moves" or "scenes." Put simply, can such image-laden, commercial-like prose truly serve the purposes of preaching in the church — the first of which is ostensibly that of communication? While we should avoid hasty conclusions, several preliminary observations are possible.

### Images and Understanding

The rhetoric of preaching shaped by intense visual media is not well suited to form a thought in the congregation's consciousness.

8

That is, language that serves up images wholesale represents a pitfall, for it leaves little or no time for any single image to serve as a catalyst for conceptual understanding. Such rhetoric, it seems, cannot function to interpret biblical texts in which a thought or a sequence of thoughts is at stake. Similarly, this rhetoric will not serve any homiletics that construes preaching as a plotted sequence of thoughts formed in the hearing of a congregation (such as Buttrick, Lowry, and Craddock have argued).

## The Power of Images

Like the commercials or MTV videos they emulate, this new approach to the sermon will quite possibly succeed in conveying a mood, an attitude, a mental and emotional "state of affairs." The effect on the hearers may well be quite powerful, resulting in deep affective states. (Images, after all, are capable of evoking strong emotions within hearers and viewers.) In fact, if a preacher really wants to evoke (or, others might add, manipulate) congregational feelings, a depiction of powerful imagery is even more effective than the traditional pathos-laden anecdote. We do have, as MTV and the advertising industry have discovered, an awesome means here for evoking feelings and perceptions about things, other persons, and ourselves.

## Imagery and Interpretation

For the most part, on those occasions when I, your Pitfalls author, have heard sermons filled with an overly rich diet of imagery, the result for the hearers has been mostly that of being boggled and confused. Part of the problem was the expectation we hearers brought to the event — we came expecting some sequence of thoughts that we could follow, some plottable logic. That expectation, clearly, was denied. However, we also were left with a mood, an attitude, a certain state of affairs.

After one such sermon, I remember that we hearers felt keenly the confused tumble of the images such as they assault us through

Do you see the Bible here?
Do you see the Word here?
lanlgouge

PITFALLS IN PREACHING

the visual media; we had been inundated with the good, the bad, and the ugly, all coming at us at once. How we were to interpret this potpourri was not addressed in the sermon. Insofar as preachers are called to frame the images of our contemporary world in biblical terms, however, this particular sermon was a failure.

What are we to do with the images of our lives when they have been intensified from the pulpit but not interpreted? This situation must first be recognized as a pitfall, and then efforts can be made to reconnect images and their interpretation.

### For further reading

Eslinger, Richard. "Narrative and Imagery." In *Intersections: Post-Critical Studies in Preaching,* ed. Richard Eslinger, pp. 65–87. Grand Rapids: Wm. B. Eerdmans Publishing Co., 1994.

Eslinger, Richard. "Narrative and Imagery in Relationship." In *Narrative and Imagination: Preaching the Worlds That Shape Us,* pp. 46–60, 76–89. Minneapolis: Fortress Press, 1995.

Lowry, Eugene. *How to Preach a Parable: Designs for Narrative Sermons.* Nashville: Abingdon Press, 1989.

## 1.4. Dark and Stormy Sermons

Edward Bulwer-Lytton was a nineteenth-century novelist whose excessive powers of description have won him a certain notoriety. His opening line "It was a dark and stormy night . . ." has been picked up by Madeleine L'Engle in her wonderful *Wind in the Door* and by the redoubtable Snoopy in Charles Schulz's *Peanuts* comic strip. In a way, Bulwer-Lytton has also been picked up by many of us preachers; perhaps he could even be considered a patron saint of modern homiletics! If you hear someone parodying "preacher-talk," it often is through using language with excessive coloration and descriptive prose.

As Eugene Lowry has noted, we have all learned in our English lit classes that adjectives are the primary means of describing something. It is therefore natural to reach for these same linguistic tools in our preaching. The problem is that adjectives do not work the same way in literary and in homiletic contexts; oral communication in a communal context is a quite different species than written prose. In fact, multiplying descriptive adjectives within a sermon actually works against its intended purpose. These adjectives, as David Buttrick observes, "clutter oral language and prevent understanding" (*Homiletic*, p. 192). In preaching, the effective tools of coloration and description are nouns and verbs, particularly when employed with imagination.

Read the two following statements aloud, listening for their respective effect:

*Zacchaeus was very short, even for people of his day. When he came to see Jesus, the large and bustling crowd was an impenetrable wall of humanity. Then a brilliant idea hit him. He carefully climbed up an old sycamore tree and sat balanced on one of its sturdy limbs.*

*Watch Zacchaeus peering over the crowd, trying to glimpse Rabbi Jesus. "No, short stuff," he tells himself, "this won't work, never does!" So there he is, out of costume for climbing trees — but look, he's hoisted himself up to that branch, and there he's perched, surveying the scene over the heads of all those common folk down below.*

The first example attempts to describe by way of increasing adjectives and adverbs. The result sounds preachy; the ideas have become foggy rather than clear. The latter employs verbal coloration, including connotative and metaphoric terms (e.g., "perch"). This descriptive strategy works fine within a communal setting, but that of the former will not. We may chart this situation as in the figure below.

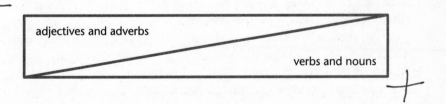

Our language of description in preaching should be located well toward the right-hand pole of this "color schema" To the left lurks a pitfall — a sort of homiletic "cotton candy" that audiences find surprisingly difficult to retain.

### For further reading

Buttrick, David. *Homiletic: Moves and Structures*, pp. 189–98. Philadelphia: Fortress Press, 1987.
Lowry, Eugene. *How to Preach a Parable: Designs for Narrative Sermons*, pp. 163–64. Nashville: Abingdon Press, 1989.

## 1.5. Doublet Demons

Some of our most popular language in the pulpit takes the form of a doublet. We hear word doublets such as "peace and justice" or "love and mercy." Doublets also occur in our use of illustrations and even in the organization of an entire sermon. We seem to like doublets and easily sprinkle them unconsciously throughout our preaching; they somehow sound sermonic.

There is a serious pitfall in the use of doublets, however; they simply do not function well in communal hearing and retention. In fact, the most likely fate of homiletic doublets is that one of the pair never forms in the hearers' minds at all! At best, only one of the two is retained. At worst, the doublet may simply blur together in the communal mind, thus losing the specific meaning and application of both elements.

With such a dire prognosis for sermonic doublets, it is important that we try to get a handle on this rhetorical pitfall. A doublet is any portion of communal speech in which two elements *of equal value* — words, images, illustrations — are paired. The matter of equal value is central to the creation of a doublet and somehow serves to hasten its demise in a congregation's hearing. For example, it is clear that "peace and justice" is a doublet according to our definition. It is also apparent how, lacking clarity of individual focus in this binary form, the doublet can become blurred together (as though we were saying "peesnjustess"). This blurred doublet might be heard as a buzzword by the hearers and provide a sense of satisfaction (or perhaps dissatisfaction) whenever it is mentioned. What will *not* be heard are the two parts of the binary pair in their individual meaning and intention.

With these cautions in mind, we will be alert to possible doublet systems latent within the biblical text. For example, we noted in section 2.2 above that the pericope in Mark 10 dealing with the request of James and John contains a doublet structure, which the preacher might be tempted to exploit. After James and John make their childish and self-centered request, Jesus replies, using two central images: drinking the cup (which suggests the Eucharist) and being able to be baptized with his baptism. The two images are perfect examples of a doublet system — they are offered as alternative means of imaging a single meaning (i.e., discipleship) and are of equal value with regard to this meaning.

It will therefore be difficult for the preacher to develop fully both images in the course of a sermon on Mark 10:35-45, particularly if the sermon is "running the narrative" (i.e., following along with the text's plot). Since we cannot attend to both images — both "the cup" and baptism — we will want to select one or the other, most likely on the basis of pastoral issues within the life of the parish. We can display the structure and movement of the pericope as in the figure on page 14. A sermon preached directly on such a text will track one of the two images wherever the doublet is presented or implied, but it will resolutely avoid the pitfall of trying to tackle both.

### For further reading

Buttrick, David. *Homiletic: Moves and Structures*, pp. 213–16. Philadelphia: Fortress Press, 1987.

Eslinger, Richard. *A New Hearing: Living Options in Homiletic Method*, chap. 5. Nashville: Abingdon Press, 1987.

## A Plotting of Mark 10:35-45

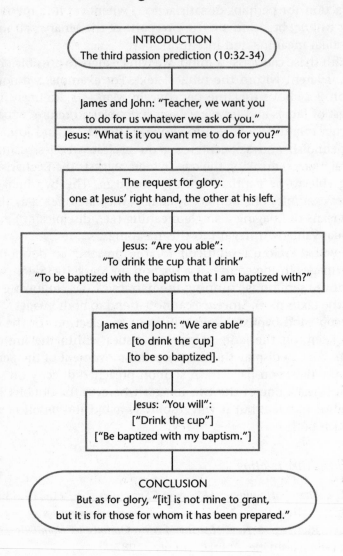

INTRODUCTION
The third passion prediction (10:32-34)

James and John: "Teacher, we want you
to do for us whatever we ask of you."
Jesus: "What is it you want me to do for you?"

The request for glory:
one at Jesus' right hand, the other at his left.

Jesus: "Are you able":
"To drink the cup that I drink"
"To be baptized with the baptism that I am baptized with?"

James and John: "We are able"
[to drink the cup]
[to be so baptized].

Jesus: "You will":
["Drink the cup"]
["Be baptized with my baptism."]

CONCLUSION
But as for glory, "[it] is not mine to grant,
but it is for those for whom it has been prepared."

## 1.6. Empty Calories

A romantic tradition within modern preaching continues to shape our pulpit language, even in this postmodern age. While we may joke with our colleagues about this "preacher style" — just as we do about the old three points and a poem — the alternatives to such stereotyped rhetoric may be unclear. The result is that we may unwittingly continue to use a language that could be described as fond (in the archaic sense of foolish or silly), syrupy, or simply "preachery." We could also dub this form of pulpit speech "empty calories," since its usage contributes nothing to communication and actually tends to drain the meaning from our communal speech.

The use of empty-calorie language is a pitfall precisely because it is such an easy trap to fall into when preaching. Without a certain level of vigilance, this romantic prose slips into our public language unintended and unnoticed. The effectiveness of our preaching suffers as a result, as interest and retention of the message decline. Use of empty, romantic prose diminishes the level of communication, even as it reinforces the stereotypes of preaching and the preacher as "religious" and slightly out of this world. All of us struggle with a cultural stereotype of our role and our message, which we do not need to reinforce by persisting in such empty-calorie rhetoric.

Stock examples of this preachery rhetoric include the well-worn adverbs "very," "truly," "really," "awfully," and "only," as well as many trendy verbs made from nouns ("to fellowship," "to dialogue," "to prioritize"). Uses of "just" are empty sermonic calories when appearing in "I just want to . . . ," whether in prayers ("I just wanna thank you, Jeeesus") or otherwise. The "sermonic subjunctive" also fits the description of empty calories: "if only we would . . ."; "if only we might . . ."; "if only we could. . . ." Filler words and phrases ("well," "like," "you know") serve only to detract from communication.

A related area involves the traditional rhetoric of pulpit imperative. Fred Craddock has repeatedly emphasized that our preaching tends to be heard as a series of "must," "ought," and "should" imperatives. Perhaps surprisingly, appeals for congregational action

15

couched in these traditional pulpit imperatives are not heard as forceful ethical speech. Rather, the form has become so stereotyped that it more commonly conveys feelings of a "being preached to" moralism. Real prophetic preaching will stay away from this "must, ought, should" kind of speech entirely.

*Hint:* Although we may recognize the harm of using empty-calorie terms, a congregation may nevertheless have a form of piety or ideological commitments that strongly call for the use of these same terms. For example, certain communities of faith have come to expect prayer and preaching to be introduced with "I just want to. . . ." In such a setting, a preacher who quits using this phrase cold turkey might very well be received as lacking in spirituality or as simply being cold and formal.

In such contexts, community expectations may temporarily override a preacher's rightful caution about avoiding this pitfall. Simply put, we may have to ante up with some jargonized usage in order to begin to be heard. Our responsibility remains, however, to use such language in the least harmful locations possible and to begin a journey with the congregation toward a more authentic form of preaching and of prayer.

*For further reading*

Craddock, Fred B. *Preaching,* pp. 196–209. Nashville: Abingdon Press, 1985.

## 1.7. Hypnotic Spells and Incantations

It is natural for oral speaking to organize itself according to rhythm, meter, and rhyme. In fact, New Testament scholars are increasingly convinced of the originally oral character of the Gospels, on the basis of the evidence of such linguistic patterns. Many of these patterns of speaking within oral discourse are remarkably helpful means of invoking tone and deepening the affective response of the hearers. (See chap. 2, "Henry Mitchell: Narrative in the Black Tradition," in my *A New Hearing.*) As with most good things, however, the power of these patterns of speech can become a pitfall.

One of the easiest ways to design language that will immediately delete from congregational hearing is to shape a series of metrically aligned phrases that all share the same pattern. Unfortunately, such hypnotic rhetoric has become a stereotyped "sermon-sounding" kind of pulpit language. Consider the following pattern:

Jesus talks to his disciples about love.
He talks to every Christian about love.
We must talk to others about love.

While the logic of the sequence is clear — a movement from Jesus to the world regarding his message of love — its shape will cause it to immediately drop from congregational consciousness. How to avoid this rhetorical pitfall? Change the recurring pattern that produces the hypnotic effect. While the first two lines may share a similar meter or rhyme, the third line must disturb it in some fashion. We could try contraction, making the tag line more terse so it no longer conforms to the emerging rhetorical pattern ("Christians talk love!"). Or we could expand it, elaborating the line beyond the frame of the rhetorical system (" 'And when you speak with each other,' Jesus adds, 'talk with love!' ").

Readers no doubt can see a connection between this little rhetorical system and hymn texts and other poetry. In fact, long quotations from such traditional sources also will not be retained in the congregational hearing. (Some affective response might occur, but not much else.) These days, preachers will have to "break apart" traditionally metered texts from hymns and poems in order for them to communicate.

Another typical pattern found within sermonic rhetoric is one ordered by fours (for example, *"The apostle Paul speaks of love and hope and righteousness and joy"*). Whether the quartets are of words or of larger units such as phrases or sentences, there is a potential pitfall lurking in the pattern. At the level of words, a fourfold pattern is simply difficult to remember. The order of the terms is easily scrambled, and the whole system tends to be forgotten. (One well-known book on worship uses a word quartet as its title. Almost inevitably, readers have trouble remembering the book's title at all, or else they get the order of the words mixed up.) The best advice for preachers is to watch for the appearance of word quartets and redo the language for better comprehension. At the level of phrases and sentences, a similar situation obtains. Clearly, the meter of such systems needs to be disrupted before the language will function as intended.

One effective use of quartet systems remains, however. If we are seeking to build a congregational sense of plenitude, or crowding at some point in the sermon, a fourfold pattern works well — but only if we do not intend at the same time to communicate every component meaning. In talking about the unity in diversity of the church, for example, we might form the following system that utilizes a quartet pattern:

> *Pilgrims to the Holy Land bump into this wonderful mix of people called church. They get off the bus and trek up to the Mount of Beatitudes. If the thought of being alone with Jesus was intended, guess what? Latino Christians are there singing a song at Mass, Germans are blaring out a chorale, some Ethiopians are all joining in a chant, and Korean Presbyterians are listening to their preacher, who's really getting excited about the Gospel.*

Notice, however, that the metered pattern of the phrases here has been intentionally altered in each successive line. Again, if we build a system sounding too much like the four lines of a traditional hymn text, the entire block of material may simply delete from congregational hearing.

Finally, under this pitfall we must include the kind of sermonic rhetoric that achieves a sing-song effect. *("What we need is that still, small voice, a voice of comfort, a voice of calm, a voice of peace, and even a voice of tranquility.")* Here, unconscious breathing patterns, perhaps mixed with an intent of producing a "spiritual effect," renders the language as predictable as waves lapping up on a beach. Just as tapes of the sound of those rhythmic waves are marketed as relaxation aids, so too preaching with an unrelieved pattern of inflection or stress is just what the doctor ordered for producing a group of very relaxed (if not sound asleep) hearers.

### For further reading

Buttrick, David. *Homiletic: Moves and Structures*, pp. 189–98. Philadelphia: Fortress Press, 1987.
Dewey, Joanna. "Oral Methods of Structuring Narrative in Mark." In *Intersections: Post-Critical Studies in Preaching*, ed. Richard Eslinger, pp. 23–41. Grand Rapids: Wm. B. Eerdmans Publishing Co., 1994.
Eslinger, Richard. *A New Hearing: Living Options in Homiletic Method*, chaps. 2 and 5. Nashville: Abingdon Press, 1987.

## 1.8. The Search for a "Preaching Style"

*Preachers would be better off . . . without a style.*

David Buttrick, *Homiletic*

"Style" is one way we label preaching, both that of ourselves and that of our colleagues. This one or that one is said to have a good preaching style. Or we speak of inheriting our own style from this or that mentor. Workshops on preaching regularly address such topics as "Forming Your Own Preaching Style."

The pitfalls here fall into two general categories. First, we may confuse style with method. The former is a matter of shaping the rhetoric appropriate for a given sermon. The latter raises the question of strategy with regard to homiletic plot, its movement and intention. To speak of narrative preaching or inductive preaching is not necessarily the same as addressing sermonic style. In fact, it is helpful *not* to speak of style in this generic sense when dealing with methodologies for preaching.

The second issue relates to our quest for a style. If we do achieve

19

a distinctive style, please notice, we are thereby assuming that all of the incredible variety of meanings and images within our preaching are susceptible to being expressed in that one style. A liturgical analogy would be the assumption that all of the forms of expression in the Psalms could be adequately rendered by a single musical setting or tune.

Rather than settling for a single style, we would be wise to accumulate an entire palette of stylistic speech, all styles available in the service of the single meaning at stake during a given move or sequence in the sermon. For example, just imagine the kind of style our speech will take as we are speaking of Jesus' invitation to "come as a child." The language will be simple, childlike in its vocabulary and its expression. In contrast, if we are developing a sermonic move dealing with Jesus' anger seen in the accounts of the temple cleansing, we will seek language that incarnates a terse, blunt kind of prose. Style, let us conclude, does not relate to our language of preaching in general. Rather, the issue of style deals with how we shape our language in each successive move within a sermon; our style will shift, according to the meanings at stake in the course of the homiletic plot.

### For further reading

Buttrick, David. *Homiletic: Moves and Structures,* pp. 199–221. Philadelphia: Fortress Press, 1987.

Craddock, Fred B. *Preaching,* 189–93. Nashville: Abingdon Press, 1985. On the importance in preaching of using oral style rather than literary style.

*Assignment:* Following Buttrick's method in *Homiletic,* develop a "move" related to each of the following scenes. Pay special attention to the style of the language employed in each one. After you have completed the moves, again check each for its style. Has the style of the language shifted appropriately with the respective meanings being expressed? Or has one "master style" flattened out the variation appropriate for these samples?

- *Look at Jesus eating and drinking with sinners, whooping it up with all the outcasts in town!*

- *Ever been out in that sea called "fear," where the wind and the waves beat against your little boat and there's no place to hide from the storm?*

- *Then the prophet turns to God's people, turns to us, "'For your three transgressions and for four, I will not hold you guiltless,' says the Lord."*

## 1.9. A Question of Questions

Preachers use questions in sermons in various ways. Most of these uses represent effective rhetorical tools, but all can lead to pitfalls. We find questions being asked of congregations at the beginning of a sermon or sermon section, as well as at the end. The preacher may build a system of rhetorical questions or even may ask factual questions during the sermon. Let's consider these various options, looking particularly for the pitfalls and pathways of each.

### At the Beginning

We may use a question to begin the sermon itself or a section within the sermon that expresses a single meaning. The material that follows the question, then, may be devoted to expanding the issue expressed by the question, or it may simply answer the opening question. In the first case, we are on solid rhetorical grounds, for we are building a whole attitude of reflective interrogation in the consciousness of the hearers. Insofar as we develop the move out of the lived experience of the people, the result will form quite nicely in the congregational hearing.

For example, if we are preparing a sermon on Mark's account of the Transfiguration (9:2-9), we might peck out a move on our word processor that develops an opening question.

> *Did you ever wonder why the voice from the overshadowing cloud says, "Listen to him"? It's odd, really . . . this divine "Listen up, you!" Mainly odd because Jesus hasn't said anything at all up here on the mountain. No, nothing to hear, but sure a lot to see. I mean, it's all vision . . . the dazzling white, Elijah and Moses, and now this overshadowing cloud. But maybe that's the point of the cloud. You can't see anything in the bright cloud. Try as hard as you can — nothing! Only those little specks running around in our eyeballs. But we can hear, where sight is fruitless up here. Like coming out of anesthesia when you were a kid and before you see anything, you hear Mom speaking love through the fog. "Listen to him!" the voice commands. Which may be roughly translated, "Get ready to hear what he has to say!"*

No pitfall here. This portion of a sermon on the Transfiguration shapes a "questioning," reflective kind of consciousness within the hearers. This perspective is retained throughout the move with its visual and aural imagery shaped by the biblical text itself.

## At the End

In contrast to its use at the beginning of a sermonic section, a question used as the tag line at the end of a section all too often encounters serious pitfalls. In some cases, the intent is to invite commitment or perhaps to try to keep the issue of the sermon open for the hearers throughout the week ahead. The pitfall here is that neither intent carries through very well. Questions placed at the end of sermons tend to delete immediately from congregational hearing. A question may be located within the body of the concluding material, provided that the other statements within the conclusion are presented with a declarative strength. We can state as a rhetorical law that ending a sermon conclusion with a question will cause that tag line and perhaps the entire conclusion to be dropped from communal consciousness. If we build a question into our conclusion, we are best advised to locate it early in the closure system.

## Rhetorical Questions

Preachers intent on creating a sermonic event of great impact will occasionally build a rhetorical unit, usually early in the sermon, based on a series of rhetorical questions. (Such units also seem to be common in sermons by preachers "running for bishop," as those of us in the Methodist tradition might put it.) While these systems based on rhetorical questions do have the potential of conveying a strong affective sense, they also face the pitfall of being easily lost from congregational consciousness. Thus, if we design a system that inventories some of the more dreadful social issues of the day (*"What do you call it when a ten-year-old child has never seen the inside of a doctor's office?" "What do you call it when an able-bodied middle-aged man has never held a decent job in his life?"* etc.), we should not expect that our five or six leading examples will all be retained. Some may stick, some not, perhaps depending on the particular experience of the hearers. Such a system does have affective power, but the preacher must use caution here. The response may be a deeply felt, "Yes, that's how it is!" In contrast, the people may have only the negative thought, "I'm really being manipulated here!"

Another factor in the use of systems of rhetorical questions is that they often function to build a unified perspective within the communal consciousness. I once noticed this dynamic clearly in a sermon, although largely because it was not observed in the overall sermon construction. The preacher was listing some "signs of the times," each prefaced with, "What do you see, church, when. . . ."

23

The various signs dealt with homelessness, hunger, and other pressing social issues. Immediately following this rhetorical system, however, the preacher brought up the old story about Pavlov's dog, involving bells ringing and learned responses. It soon became apparent to me that few in the assembled community got anything out of the entire system of rhetorical questions. Why? After building a strong visual point of view (by asking, "What do you *see*, church . . ."), the preacher shifted to a strong auditory perspective. The change of focus from sight to hearing was too rapid for the hearers to make. They later commented, "Oh, he really preached!" I noted, though, that *what* was preached remained quite vague to them.

*A pathway for questions:* Ronald Allen lists two criteria for the effective use of questions in a sermon. First, "they should be specific. They should relate to specific persons, occasions, ideas, or practices." With this in mind, to begin with the question, "How shall we find hope in our present age?" probably puts us back in the pit. Second, "the questions should move from the particular to the general." By this, Allen means that we invite our hearers to ponder a specific question and move to more general considerations once that question has been heard in its concretion. Allen's example here is that the preacher might first question what to say to a person terminally ill with cancer, and to her family. Only after this situation is explored concretely should the preacher then question how to speak of God as both loving and just. (Ronald J. Allen, *The Teaching Sermon* [Nashville: Abingdon Press, 1995], p. 47.)

## *"Real" Questions*

A practice heard increasingly in sermons today involves the use of "real" rather than rhetorical questions. The preacher may be poised to illustrate some single meaning in the sermon — for example, by referring to a movie — and may preface it by asking, "How many here saw *Unforgiven,* with Clint Eastwood?" A number of hands will be dutifully raised in the congregation, while some may show by their facial expressions that they have never even heard of the film.

In other instances, a question will be raised for which the preacher possesses the right answer ahead of time. *"In a recent poll, people were asked if they would wear a sweater owned and worn by Adolf Hitler. Most everybody said they would not wear it. Now the pollster asked: 'If that sweater were unraveled and knitted into a completely different sweater, would you wear it now?' How many here think that folks said they would wear it? . . . How many that they wouldn't?"* In this case, the preacher knew ahead of time that the vast majority

---

*Hint:* A preacher may introduce a kind of reflectivity among the assembly by taking a kind of "Lieutenant Columbo" stance with regard to questions. Thus we might interrogate the text's character or its position on an issue. Such questions could begin, "Now let me get this straight . . . we're not only *not* to strike back, but we're to turn the other cheek too?" or "Now I don't know about you, but this confuses me. I mean, why would Jesus heal this man on the Sabbath?"

We will not want to lengthen unduly such questions. After all, we're not trying to convey the idea that the preacher is hopelessly confused in the sermon today! (Eugene Lowry has extended this reflective and questioning stance before the text into an entire homiletic method; see his *Homiletical Plot.*)

of those polled indicated that they would not wear the re-knit apparel.

In such interchanges between pulpit and congregation, there is an attempt at deeper intimacy in communication. The preacher may feel more closely connected to his or her people in such question-and-answer sermonic interludes. Apart from what the preacher intends or feels, however, the practice itself is rife with problems and pitfalls. Those who give the wrong answer will most likely feel put down or rejected. In fact, the whole question-and-answer format may stir up some really negative or painful feelings for the people as they remember times from their elementary school days when they gave wrong answers in class. There is a further potential for problem when this method is used repeatedly in our preaching. People in the congregation will soon tire of raising and lowering their hands. Also, they may soon begin to resent the process, thinking, "I am being manipulated by all these questions!"

Fortunately, there are other, much more effective methods for establishing the kind of contact and dialogue sought by the question-asking preacher. Provide images out of the lived experience of the hearers, and develop a strong point of view. In short, we can dispense with the practice of asking "real" questions and expecting "real" answers without any negative consequences whatsoever.

### For further reading

Long, Thomas G. *The Witness of Preaching*, pp. 195–98. Louisville, Ky.: Westminster/John Knox Press, 1989.

Lowry, Eugene. *The Homiletical Plot: The Sermon as Narrative Art Form.* Atlanta: John Knox Press, 1980.

Tolbert, Mary Ann. *Sowing the Gospel: Mark's World in Literary and Historical Perspective.* Minneapolis: Fortress Press, 1989.

# 2. Scripture and Interpretation

A major shift has occurred in scriptural interpretation since the 1960s. The earlier orthodoxy of interpretation sought to identify a text's themes or treated the text as a window to an ancient world. Now biblical interpreters examine a text for its literary form, for its movement and structure. The former "static" model of seeking main ideas from a text has given way to a "fluid" interest in a text's movement and intentionality. Other interpreters now look for the text's commitments for or against human liberation, while still others attempt to deconstruct any text's narrative world, arguing that it cannot convey meaning and security in this postmodern world.

The new approaches to interpretation — literary criticism, reader-response criticism, and liberation theology — have already yielded a rich harvest of theological insight and much lively debate and conversation. It is a turbulent and even chaotic time for hermeneutics. For all its diversity, however, one conclusion is clear: we cannot return to the familiar position of Enlightenment rationalism. Both for biblical interpretation and for preaching, the pathway lies only ahead.

## 2.1. Slow-Cooking Preachers

*Preachers are not merely to look for theological
ideas floating in a historical soup.*

Thomas G. Long, "The Preacher and the Beast:
From Apocalyptic Text to Sermon"

Imagine that you have come to a workshop on preaching. After
coffee, doughnuts, and the usual introductions, the first session
begins. A sheet of paper is distributed to each participant containing
Mark's text of "The Request of James and John" (10:35-45). "Now,"
begins the instructor, "the question is what we see in this text that
can be preached. I'll be the scribe, and you just call out what you
find." You and the other workshop members respond, and within
a few minutes there is a list on the chalkboard containing the
following phrases:

We are able
The cup of sorrow
A request for glory
The inevitability of suffering
True glory
The Father's secret
A Christian's true baptism
The real meaning of the Lord's Supper
Discipleship = Servanthood

After writing all the ideas, the workshop leader observes wryly,
"Well, colleagues, we've just done it again. Probably for the mil-
lionth time, we've taken a biblical text, and in order to 'process' it
for preaching, we've put it in a slow-cooker and boiled it down until
only conceptual themes are left in the bottom of the pot. The form
and movement of the text have been all boiled away. All we're left
with is themes that sound like sermon titles."

Reflecting on the workshop's opening session, we note first just
how unconscious this "slow-cooking the text" tendency has become
for us preachers. The assumptions underlying this approach to
Scripture include two sweeping, if obsolete, tenets of biblical inter-

28

pretation: first, that the literary form of the text is irrelevant to its meaning and ultimately disposable; second, that the significant payoff of almost any biblical text is some sort of discursive main idea. That is what the preacher is to detect in his or her studies. This approach furthermore assumes that the original intent of the biblical writer was to transmit a rationalistic "point."

We can shift the metaphor, noting David Buttrick's phrase "hermeneutic of distillation." By this phrase, he suggests that the interpreter all too often conceives of the text as a sort of still-life painting. The preacher-interpreter goes to the text and notices certain thoughts or themes, just as certain objects may be identified within the painting. Once an object is spotted, it is then lifted out of its context and analyzed independently. For example, a book is seen in the painting. "Oh, good!" exclaims the viewer, "I can preach on God's Word." The composition of the painting, the relationship and interaction of the various objects in the picture, has been ignored. Similarly, once the preacher extracts the theme from the text, he or she deems the form and movement of the pericope to be irrelevant. Whether the image is that of slow-cooking a text or of distilling it, the pitfall for preachers is the same. Form is essential to the meaning of a biblical text; it is neither optional nor disposable in faithful interpretation.

The alternative is to see a scriptural text as a dynamic form of language, inviting the reader/hearer along in its journey through a succession of "locations," or scenes. Buttrick invites us to imagine the text as consisting of a series of frames, like a film. None of the individual frames can be snipped out and held up as the real meaning of the whole. Each frame produces meaning in context, as an integral part of a succession of frames.

Preaching that goes beyond the constraints of the old hermeneutic of slow-cooking or distillation, a style that originated in the Enlightenment and is now finally giving way to other interpretive models, will be different. Now the preacher needs to develop a sermon with a dynamic quality, one that intentionally shapes language to track meanings-in-sequence as the congregation listens. Preaching today relies less and less on sermonic points, because such points are related to the distillation approach, which focuses on the extracted theme or main idea. The outline of the old topical preaching is giving way to the notion of homiletic plot. "Doing space," as Eugene Lowry puts it, is being replaced by "doing time."

By the end of the afternoon session, workshop participants have discovered a very different way to interpret the Markan account of the sons of Zebedee pericope. A new list on the chalkboard now contains the following entries:

— James and John ask for glory ("When you come in glory, grant us to sit, one at your right and one at your left").
— Jesus responds, "Can you drink the cup . . . or be baptized with my baptism?"
— "We are able," the disciples answer cheerily.
— "You will drink the cup I drink," Jesus announces, "and be baptized with my baptism."
— "As for glory," Jesus adds, "that is not for me to grant, . . . nor for you to know."

The session ends with this comment from the instructor: "Now that we have this surface-level analysis of the movement and form of the text, what would a sermon structure look like based upon this analysis? Work on it tonight, and we'll look at your ideas in the morning."

---

*Assignment:* Check out David Buttrick's description of the plots and intentions of biblical texts, along with an approach to preaching, in his *Homiletic: Moves and Structures* (Philadelphia: Fortress Press, 1987), pp. 285–363. Then form a homiletic plot related to this story of the sons of Zebedee.

P.S.: In "The Request of James and John," watch out for the pair "cup" and "baptism" (see secs. 1.5 and 4.1). In your sermon plot, you will need to develop one or the other, but probably not both. Which will you choose? Why?

*For further reading*

Buttrick, David. *A Captive Voice: The Liberation of Preaching*, pp. 80–88. Louisville, Ky.: Westminster/John Knox Press, 1994.

Eslinger, Richard. *A New Hearing: Living Options in Homiletic Method*, chap. 5. Nashville: Abingdon Press, 1987.

Lowry, Eugene. *Doing Time in the Pulpit: The Relationship between Narrative and Preaching*, pp. 11–28. Nashville: Abingdon Press, 1985.

Tolbert, Mary Ann. *Sowing the Gospel: Mark's World in Literary and Historical Perspective*. Minneapolis: Fortress Press, 1989.

## 2.2. Water-Skimming Birds

*The competent reader struggles to pay close attention to the text itself in all its literary and linguistic details, and is aware of its full literary context.*

Gene M. Tucker, "Reading and
Preaching the Old Testament"

Closely related to the slow-cooking approach, a water-skimming bird approaches the biblical text from above; it hovers over its surface, looking for an idea to preach. When this fowl spots one, it swoops down and plucks the idea or concept from the sea of the text without even getting wet. This bird views the text as simply a container for the idea and as therefore irrelevant to its interest once it has plucked away the idea it spotted.

In local and churchly traditions where the text is under the full control of the preacher and where "text" usually means a single verse, this pitfall is especially prevalent. Although preachers would generally agree that almost each individual verse of Scripture needs to be seen in light of its context in order to be understandable, many of us step into the pulpit and announce, "My text for this morning is . . . ," and then read only a brief segment of the total pericope (i.e., a section of the text that retains an essential unity and literary coherence when it is lifted from its larger context). This

31

practice almost ensures the water-skimming-bird approach to biblical interpretation, a practice that results in the dislocation of text from context. This practice becomes especially problematic when the preacher tries to deal with rather discursive texts such as those presented in the Pauline Epistles.

In order to avoid this pitfall in preaching, I encourage water-skimming birds to land on the text's surface and feel its movement and direction. They should even consider plunging beneath the surface, in the manner of some enterprising waterfowl.

As a test case, let's look specifically at epistolary texts for a pathway to interpretation that avoids this pitfall. While Paul's letters don't usually present a narrative kind of logic (although portions of them in fact demonstrate a narrative kind of thinking), Paul consistently offers some kind of logic or other. In all cases, the apostle's "convictional system," as Daniel Patte has termed it, is dynamic, practical, and oriented toward transformation.

By *dynamic*, I mean that Paul's writing has the form of an argument that we may trace. There is a "this, . . . therefore that" and "not this, . . . therefore not that" kind of reasoning, with component steps and stages that may be plotted.

By *practical*, I mean that Paul often presents his conclusions as part of a larger effort in a kind of Christian pedagogy. The apostle is anxious to bring the "children" to whom he writes into Christian adulthood. He typically approaches ethical issues from this practical perspective, inviting readers to find the appropriate and mature response along with him. (For an example of this practical, plottable kind of reasoning, look at Paul's grappling with the issue of meat-eating and the weaker brothers and sisters in 1 Corinthians 8.)

By *oriented toward transformation*, I refer to the way particular arguments in Paul's writings reflect his fundamental conviction that the transformation of all things is achieved through the death and resurrection of Jesus Christ. We see this conviction in microcosm in almost every sentence Paul writes (e.g., in 1 Thess. 2:1-16). These "microtransformations" are instructive to the reader regarding the particulars of Christian faith, yet they always are based on the fundamental transformations achieved "in Christ" — namely, the changes from death to life, law to Gospel, flesh to spirit, and so on. It isn't possible to "preach Paul" by extracting ideas out of context from his letters chiefly because he at all times presents a convictional system that embodies and promotes the mystery of transformation through Jesus Christ. Truly biblical preaching of the Epistles, therefore, is violated by extracting biblical texts and treating them as ideas apart from their location within a dynamic and transformative system of convictions. To preach Paul biblically requires that we design homiletic plots that seek to encourage the transformations that the apostle himself identified, and that we do so within the contemporary situation of our Christian assemblies. These plots will be mobile (dynamic) and will reflect a practical approach to discursive thought; they will highlight a system of transformation that includes the details of our Christian life and work.

*Hint:* Be aware of the difference between hearing a text and simply reading it. A merely visual relationship with a pericope may encourage both distance and thematic extraction (i.e., water-skimming). The Epistles, however, were written to be read — and were read to be heard! If we treat them as aural events, we will find a much more intimate relationship to the text in which its dynamic nature is emphasized. Furthermore, we will tend not merely to hear the ideas but to listen for the text's logic and structured intention.

Therefore, find ways to *hear* the Scripture lesson and not merely *read* it. Listen to the text as read by another person or as reproduced on an audio tape. Frame the text as an event of speech and hearing. Restoring the Word to speech will significantly reduce the temptation to water-skim.

*For further reading*

Craddock, Fred B. *Preaching,* esp. chap. 9, "The Formation of the Sermon." Nashville: Abingdon Press, 1985.

Keck, Leander E. "Romans in the Pulpit: Form and Formation in Romans 5–11." In *Listening to the Word: Studies in Honor of Fred B. Craddock,* ed. Gail R. O'Day and Thomas G. Long, pp. 77–90. Nashville: Abingdon Press, 1993.

Patte, Daniel. *Preaching Paul.* Philadelphia: Fortress Press, 1984.

Pogoloff, Stephen M. *Logos and Sophia: The Rhetorical Situation of First Corinthians.* Atlanta: Scholars Press, 1992. This work assumes some knowledge of Koine Greek.

## 2.3. Isolated Beauties

Consider a preacher who has decided to speak on the parable of the prodigal son (Luke 15:11-32). One on the prowl for an "isolated beauty" might find that the phrase "he came to himself" in verse 17 virtually leaps off the page. This experience could all too easily lead to a sermon that was based on only these four words of the entire text. Most likely, our preacher would speak of the conversion of the younger son expressed in these words, and of the need for the hearers to "come to themselves." However, if he or she focuses solely on this isolated beauty, the entire, incredibly rich narrative of this parable will probably be jettisoned as excess homiletic baggage. The preacher most likely would not venture into a consideration of the older son and his need for conversion. Moreover, by focusing solely on the younger son's coming to himself, our preacher may miss later intimations that this "conversion" was less than complete. This son's homecoming "tape" in fact has more than a little suggestion of continued interest in controlling things and people; he rehearses the script in verses 18-19 and then plays back only part of it to his father in verse 21.

While the younger son showed a continuing interest in control even after coming to himself, this pitfall of taking a text out of context assumes an approach to Scripture that is likewise un-

34

balanced as far as control is concerned. Frequently, we hear such a preacher speak of "breaking open the text," implying that some message or topic is hidden within the verse. One issue here becomes precisely that of control. Does the preacher exercise control over the text by first selecting it out of its context and then proceeding to "break it open"? If so, there are problems.

The first problem — which we have already examined above in sections 2.1 and 2.2 — is that in narrative contexts, once the "text" is extracted, the narrative itself is regarded as dispensable. The practice of preaching from such a text has resulted in a profound diminishment in the availability of biblical narrative within the churches when "text" is understood as a verse of Scripture, or even a portion of a verse. This "eclipse of biblical narrative" (Hans Frei) has become a major problem within many American churches. Usually the practice of preaching from such a text exists also in liturgical contexts where the Scripture reading is understood as providing such a text for the preacher. Oddly, this practice is prevalent too in churches claiming an evangelical heritage within the Reformation tradition. (The Reformers, though, would be appalled at such diminishment of Scripture reading within corporate worship.)

The second problem is that biblical texts construed as a single verse within a narrative generally do not retain their narrative function when separated from their context. The preacher thus speaks of "breaking open a text" because that text now lacks its proper narrative home. Meanings found as the text is "cracked open" often will be brought *to* the verse rather than extracted *from* it.

Can we agree, then, that verses of Scripture "mean something" primarily within the context of their literary form? If so, the literary form is indispensable to the way in which a scriptural text functions in the people's hearing. Perhaps we can also agree that Scripture is read first and foremost in Sunday worship for the community's edification. The preacher's role, then, is to preach from the Scriptures that the laity already have welcomed and received as their own and to do so in a way that sets each isolated beauty solidly within its proper context.

35

> *Hint:* The ability to locate the structure and movement of a biblical text is an acquired skill. Honing that skill means resisting the temptation to look at random verses of Scripture in order to find a "text" to extract. It also means becoming increasingly attentive to the movement and demonstrable logic of the entire pericope.
>
> Of all the literary forms in Scripture, parables perhaps most readily yield a series of discrete scenes. Look at the three parables of Luke 15 (the Lost Sheep, the Lost Coin, and the Lost Son) and identify the scenes that make up each story. Then compare your analysis with that of Pheme Perkins in *Hearing the Parables of Jesus,* which uses the technical word "lexie" for these essential locations of meaning in the story-world of each parable.

## *For further reading*

Buttrick, David. *A Captive Voice: The Liberation of Preaching,* pp. 76–99. Louisville, Ky.: Westminster/John Knox Press, 1994.

Frei, Hans. *The Eclipse of Biblical Narrative: A Study of Eighteenth- and Nineteenth-Century Hermeneutics.* New Haven: Yale University Press, 1974.

Perkins, Pheme. *Hearing the Parables of Jesus.* New York: Paulist Press, 1981.

## 2.4. World Builders

Imagine hearing the following paragraphs in three different sermons or homilies:

> *So the little boy Jesus looked down from the sand dune outside his little hamlet of Nazareth, watching the camel train wend its way down to Egypt. As he watched, he wondered what lay beyond the comfortable borders of his native home.*

*As Thomas saw his Lord standing there, saw the wounds in Jesus' hands and side, he finally realized that his Master really wanted just one thing — that Thomas know Jesus in his heart. And Thomas now just wanted to have his Lord dwell there deep down inside.*

*So who wants Jesus on the cross with all that messy blood and stuff? It was a shame, but not a sacrifice. No, what is really enduring about Jesus is the way we see him standing up for justice in his encounters with others, modeling inclusiveness, and enabling the marginalized toward wholeness.*

These sermon excerpts obviously represent radically different pictures of the identity of Jesus — and consequently of Christian life and work. The first one reflects the perspective of late nineteenth-century liberalism, with its interest in discovering the life of Jesus. The so-called lives of Jesus that were recovered, however, failed to provide much more than a projection of Victorian values and virtues. The "little boy Jesus" of the sermon is really an inquisitive liberal of the period about to begin a journey in the quest for Truth.

The second paragraph, with its dramatic portrayal of Thomas, reveals a deeply pietistic commitment to individualism and to internal feeling as the litmus test of Christian faith. It doesn't matter for this picture that, according to the fourth gospel, discipleship is marked by public witness *(martyria)*, along with confession of Jesus as Son of God and an abiding in communal relationship with the Good Shepherd. For this preacher, the religion of the heart is enough.

The last excerpt shows an interest in a radical feminist position, rejecting any interest in atonement. This preacher celebrates Jesus by virtue of his ministry of justice and his commitment to inclusiveness, bypassing the fact that the Jesus of the four gospels held other commitments and that his Gospel embodies both an inclusive appeal as well as a particularist claim. Justice, in this preacher's telling, is the overriding virtue for Jesus and for us. (On this subject, see also sec. 2.8, " 'The' Primary Virtue.")

Interestingly, as wildly different as the respective worlds of these three preachers are, they actually share a common model of interpretation. They all assume that a biblical text may yield a world behind the text into which interpreters may freely leap and about which they may freely discourse. All of these preachers treat the biblical text as a window rather than a mirror, looking "through" the text rather than "at" the text. That, in fact, is the pitfall into which all of them have fallen.

The modern history of homiletics has consistently celebrated "historical imagination" — the imaginative ability to take hearers behind the biblical text into the world to which it refers and there elaborate details of character, setting, and tone. Preachers have been encouraged to exercise their historical imaginations in order to portray the world behind the text in all its vividness and color. The payoff, it is assumed, is that the hearers will also leap more readily into the world of real-life Bible characters and will be able to notice their motives, thoughts, and feelings. In attempting to articulate these intangible elements, however, we find ourselves heading straight toward one of preaching's more prevalent pitfalls.

Informed portrayal of the world of the text is a valuable, even necessary, tool of effective preaching. When we preach on the parable of the lost coin (Luke 15:8-10), for example, it is helpful to know the details of the small, dark houses of the poor in first-century Palestine and to understand the social context of widows in Jewish culture. We can gain new insight into the Lukan birth narrative once we learn of the socially disreputable status of shepherds. All kinds of geographic, cultural, and even meteorologic insights into the world of Scripture are now available and will prove helpful in countless ways in the course of our preaching.

The pitfall is not here. Rather, it is in the assumption that we can go "into" the text to draw out such hidden things as a biblical character's feelings, thoughts, or motives — or, more critically, the details of authorial intention. When we assign a definite motivation to a biblical character ("the reason Zacchaeus wanted to see Jesus in the first place was . . ." or "Jesus told this parable because he wanted us to understand that . . ."), we are moving perilously near a homiletic pit. And when we announce that "the little boy Jesus sat on a sand dune outside his native hamlet of Nazareth, wondering why all men weren't brothers," we are preaching from the pit itself.

38

*For further reading*

Brown, Raymond. *The Birth of the Messiah: A Commentary on the Infancy Narratives in Matthew and Luke.* Garden City, N.Y.: Image Books, 1979.

Buttrick, David. *Homiletic: Moves and Structures,* pp. 263–81. Philadelphia: Fortress Press, 1987.

Petersen, Norman. *Literary Criticism for New Testament Critics.* Philadelphia: Fortress Press, 1978.

## 2.5. The New Dualism

To understand the next pitfall — what Edward Farley has called the new dualism — we first need to be clear about what a *paradigm* is. Think of a paradigm as a vast net thrown into the water that catches all the fish, big and little. Or a paradigm is like a pair of tinted eyeglasses that everyone in a given culture or subculture wears. The lenses filter out certain colors and objects while admitting others, but nothing that is perceived escapes being filtered. John McClure speaks of a paradigm as "a tradition of concepts, examples, and assumptions" (*The Four Codes of Preaching,* p. 74). To this notion of a tradition of interpretation, Garrett Green adds the element of imagination, speaking of a paradigm as an imaginative construct (*Imagining God,* p. 66). To use one more metaphor, think of a paradigm as imagination itself — a way of patterning and construing the world, of locating all stories, all imagery, all human action and possibility.

Once we grasp the nature of a paradigm as an overarching scheme of interpretation, then we preachers need to be especially alert to the ways in which certain paradigms shape, select, and alter our proclamation. The contemporary American church currently supports two significant paradigms that embrace self, church, and world. Although the two are mutually exclusive, they are often forced together into what Farley has called the new dualism.

One paradigm is the native-born individualism of American culture, which focuses on the rights, values, and destiny of the individual. This pervasive individualism has formed much of modern Protestant piety and polity. As analyzed by Robert Bellah in *Habits of the Heart*, the paradigm of individualism is the dominant mode of interpretation within the American culture and the American church. This individualistic paradigm accounts for much of the preaching in American churches in this century. For example, almost every sermon by Norman Vincent Peale champions the individual.

The other paradigm has emerged more recently. It views institutions as more real than individual selves and therefore standing more in need of analysis and remedy. Farley has called this more recent perspective "social-ism," written with a hyphen to distinguish it from Marxism, but still making clear its social and institutional bias. While the former paradigm may be found almost anywhere in grassroots religion in the United States, social-ism occupies a minority position in the churches but has often gained the ascendancy in denominational bureaucracies, ecumenical agencies, and theological education. The preaching of adherents of social-ism remains mostly focused on institutional power and its propensity to oppress. The call, logically, is to resist that power and to redeem those institutions. Perhaps the clearest statement of preaching within this paradigm is Christine M. Smith's *Preaching as Weeping, Confession, and Resistance*. The cover of this book lists an impressive string of isms to be exposed and resisted: "Handicapism, Ageism, Heterosexism, Sexism, White Racism, Classism."

From the perspective of biblical faith, each of these paradigms presents a partial and necessarily distorted portrayal of God-given human life. Preaching that reflects only individualism has two defects. First, it tends to minimize or ignore altogether the inherently communal character of Christian existence, as this is meant to occur in the church, the body of Christ. Second, individualism presents a truncated view of human evil and redemption. Certainly sin resides in individual human hearts, and certainly the Gospel addresses individuals with the call to repentance. But Scripture also portrays evil as communal and even transcendent. The apostle Paul, for example, calls attention to our struggle against "principalities and powers" (see 1 Cor. 15:24 and elsewhere), which can deeply enslave individuals yet can also be profoundly social. (The Holocaust comes to mind here.)

Preaching that reflects only social-ism, however, also involves bias and distortion. If evil is named only in part, then redemption will be only partially understood. As much as institutions need to be confronted and forced to change, so also individuals must face their own involvement in evil.

Therefore, preaching that abides uncritically within only one or the other of these two paradigms is inevitably going to distort the biblical narrative. For American preachers, pitfalls reside both in individualism and in social-ism. Rather than choosing which side of the new dualism to favor, preachers must plan to draw from both paradigms.

> **Example:** For a classic example of preaching out of the paradigm of individualism, see the sermon given by Norman Vincent Peale in President Richard M. Nixon's "White House Church" on June 15, 1969, reprinted in *White House Sermons*, ed. Ben Hibbs (New York: Harper & Row, 1972), pp. 55–61. For several examples of social-ism's approach to preaching, see Christine M. Smith's *Preaching as Weeping, Confession, and Resistance: Radical Responses to Radical Evil* (Louisville, Ky.: Westminster/John Knox Press, 1992), pp. 163–77.

## For further reading

Buttrick, David. *The Mystery and the Passion: A Homiletic Reading of the Gospel Traditions*, pp. 95–107. Minneapolis: Fortress Press, 1992.

Eslinger, Richard. *Narrative and Imagination: Preaching the Worlds That Shape Us*, pp. 104–9. Minneapolis; Fortress Press, 1995.

Farley, Edward. "Praxis and Piety: Hermeneutics beyond the New Dualism." In *Justice and the Holy: Essays in Honor of Walter Harrelson*, ed. Douglas A. Knight and Peter J. Paris, pp. 239–55. Atlanta: Scholars Press, 1989. Also see Farley's book *Good and Evil: Interpreting the Human Condition* (Minneapolis: Fortress Press, 1990).

Green, Garrett. *Imagining God: Theology and the Religious Imagination.* New York: Harper & Row, 1989.

McClure, John. *The Four Codes of Preaching: Rhetorical Strategies.* Minneapolis: Fortress Press, 1991.

Wink, Walter. *Naming the Powers: The Language of Power in the New Testament.* Philadelphia: Fortress Press, 1984. Also see Wink's *Unmasking the Powers* (Minneapolis: Fortress Press, 1986) and *Engaging the Powers* (Minneapolis: Fortress Press, 1992).

## 2.6. Bible Translator Games

In the 1980s I read an article entitled "Games Bible Translators Play." In it, the author noted a consistent bias in Bible translations that diminished, or even eliminated, the rightful mention of women in the text. Such an observation seems to have been noted, for more recent translations and paraphrases are, on the whole, much more sensitive to the issue of women's presence in Scripture, as well as to the whole matter of language and gender. Unfortunately, not all recent translations have followed suit, plus we still have to contend with the old King James Version, the text underlying our communal memory as a people of faith.

While gender issues have received considerable attention, other persistent questions of translation have often been ignored. Although I do not assume that all preachers are competent in the original languages of Scripture (and even such knowledge is not an absolute protection against all problems), it is nevertheless essential that we recognize various pitfalls of paraphrases and translations. In this section I mention four, giving some examples of each.

### Wrong Word Again!

In certain instances, a bad choice in word translation throws off our best attempts at interpretation. For example, translators variously render the word *zume* as "yeast" or "leaven" throughout the Synoptic Gospels, most particularly in the parable of the leaven

(Matt. 13:33/Luke 13:21) and in Jesus' reference to the leaven of the Pharisees in Mark 8:15. In all of these cases, to use the word "yeast" is to invite a pedestrian or even misleading reading of the text. While "yeast" may conjure up pleasant memories of the aroma of homemade bread rising in grandmother's kitchen, it in no way shares in the cognitive or affective meaning of the biblical "leaven."

As Bernard Brandon Scott observes, "yeast" lacks all of the associations that are essential to the meaning of "leaven," including corruption, evil, and that which is unclean. It is "rotten bread and has a strong smell" (*The Word of God in Words,* p. 23). The opposite of "leaven" is "unleavened," as in the absence of corruption essential to Israel's Feast of Unleavened Bread. In both Testaments, "leaven" retains a connotation of that which is vile, unclean, and corrupt.

Now, with the help of Scott and others, wrestle anew with the parable of the leaven, noting that the woman "hides" the leaven in the dough until the whole lump is leavened (see Scott, *Hear Then the Parable,* pp. 321–29). Also, note that translations that use "mixes" instead of "hides" tend to defang the power of this text.

### *Ideology Lives!*

Regrettably, ideological interests still intrude powerfully into the task of translation. Some of the more grievous examples of bias are particularly evident in recent attempts at paraphrase. In this respect, neither the paraphrases of the evangelical extreme nor those of the liberal extreme have much to commend themselves over against each other. For whatever reasons, the paraphrasers of the Living Bible chose to translate *logos* as "Christ," not the normal "Word," in the prologue of the fourth gospel. John 1:1 has been rendered, "Before anything else existed, there was Christ, with God." (The Living Bible seems to specialize in christological confusion. "Son of Humanity" becomes "Messiah" or simply disappears in favor of a simple pronoun reference — "he" or "me.") In this irresponsible decision, the editors have distorted John's programmatic hymn to the Word, who was with God and was God, and yet became flesh and dwelt among us. (See Paul Minear, *John,* pp. 92–102.)

On the other side of the scale, *The Inclusive Language Lectionary,* in its zeal to recover the place of women within the text, has generalized the man born blind in John 9. In its telling, this male has become simply "the person born blind."

In offering these criticisms, I don't mean to suggest that paraphrases have less intrinsic value than more "literal" biblical translations. In fact, some words and expressions in Hebrew and Greek are best served by contemporary paraphrase, in which translators seek to reproduce what has been called the "dynamic equivalence" of the original meaning, as opposed to settling for mere "formal correspondence." Perhaps the conclusion here is that paraphrase is more susceptible to both exceptional success and lamentable abuse.

### "Underwhelming" Texts

For some reason, Bible translators seem skittish around certain strong emotional terms in the original. Perhaps these scholars are influenced by a perception that English words for these powerful emotions would be inappropriate in our rather restrained Sunday or church contexts. Whatever the reason, verbs in the gospel narratives that speak of strong negative feelings are usually rendered by much-tamed English alternates. Our preaching most likely will not convey the power of the states of feeling expressed in biblical narratives if, for example, we only have such tame phrases as "deeply moved" to translate *tarassein,* "cause acute emotional distress or turbulence," used of Jesus in John 11:33, 12:27, and 13:21. (See my *Narrative and Imagination,* pp. 149–51, for a discussion of the homiletic implications of these strong biblical verbs.)

### Arius Again

In certain liberal Protestant contexts, it has become the routine practice — all in the name of inclusiveness — to delete "Father" as a reference to God and to substitute "Creator." So if we were worshiping in one of these communities, we would hear from Matthew's Sermon on the Mount that "your heavenly Creator knows that you need all these things" (6:32). Rendering the text "inclusive" here clearly shifts its meaning away from the original image of parental lovingkindness and mercy. This process reflects what we could call a Living Bible mentality, in which references to God and Christ can be adjusted at will to suit the piety and ideology of the respective worship leaders.

When this kind of substitution is made in readings from the fourth gospel, it is not simply a case of bad translation — it is a case of bad theology or, more accurately, heretical theology. The problem stems from the way in which the Greek word *pater* (father) functions in the Gospel of John. Here the term "father" does not mean "heavenly Parent," as it usually does in Matthew. Rather, in the fourth gospel, "Father" is consistently employed to locate and qualify the relationship between Jesus and the One who sends him into the world. Jesus is the Son; that One is the Father. The former is sent by the latter, knows all that the latter knows, abides in the latter's love, and receives those believers bestowed by the latter. The New Testament theological roots of the "economic" dimensions of the Holy Trinity reside largely in these texts.

Now notice what happens when "Father" becomes "Creator" with regard to the Word made flesh. The Prologue's witness to the eternity of the Word and the generativity of the Word are both overthrown in the word shift. "What's wrong with all that?" someone might ask. Two things. First, when "Father" is replaced with "Creator," John's gospel is forced to say that which it precisely opposes — that the Son is created, the notion espoused by Arius. Orthodoxy champions the principle, "If the Son is created, he cannot save." Second, once the Word made flesh is given the status of creature alongside all the rest of creation, the Word's work of redemption, as well as of creation, is diminished, if not thwarted altogether. Amazingly, this "innocent" shift in how we name God can transform the Gospel of John into a book that Arius would love.

### For further reading

Eslinger, Richard. *Narrative and Imagination: Preaching the Worlds That Shape Us.* Minneapolis: Fortress Press, 1995. See pp. 149–51 for a discussion of the "simulator model" of imaging in the sermon, relevant for handling the strong emotional verbs of the original languages.

González, Justo L., and Catherine G. González. *The Liberating Pulpit*. Nashville: Abingdon Press, 1994. See esp. pp. 35–41 for a discussion of several of the pitfalls related to Bible translation.

Lacugna, Catherine Mowry. *God for Us: The Trinity and Christian Life*. San Francisco: HarperSanFrancisco, 1991. See chap. 1 for an excellent discussion of Trinitarian thought before Nicaea and the Arian controversy.

Minear, Paul. *John: The Martyr's Gospel*. New York: Pilgrim Press, 1984.

Scott, Bernard Brandon. *Hear Then the Parable: A Commentary on the Parables of Jesus*. Minneapolis: Fortress Press, 1989.

Scott, Bernard Brandon. *The Word of God in Words*. Philadelphia: Fortress Press, 1985.

## 2.7. Generic Infection

We can distinguish several degrees of distance between sermons and the biblical text, the furthest of which is the pitfall of "generic infection" (John McClure's term).

The most direct form of preaching is what David Buttrick has called preaching in the mode of *immediacy,* where the movement and structure of the biblical pericope become the movement and structure of the sermon itself.

For an example of such a sermon, read chapters 7–9 in the Book of Genesis and then turn to Dennis Willis's sermon "Noah Was a Good Man," reprinted in Eugene Lowry's *How to Preach a Parable,* pp. 42–49. Notice the way in which the sermon directly reflects the movement of the biblical narrative. Lowry labels this approach to narrative preaching "running the story." (See Lowry's valuable commentary on Willis's sermon and narrative method on pp. 49–78.)

A bit further removed from the text is the sermon preached in the mode of *reflection.* Here we may ponder what the text is doing or asserting, question some discrepancy within the text, or simply reflect with our hearers in awe at what is going on in the text.

Some sermons may travel along in close alignment with the plot of the biblical text yet at certain points move off into more reflection. Other sermons may be shaped entirely with the reflective mode. In either case, however, the mode of preaching remains fully within the theological field of Scripture. This mode appears, for example, in a sequence of moves in my sermon entitled "Storm in the Boat," in *Narrative and Imagination,* pp. 186–93. (Notice that the sermon's initial moves are in the mode of immediacy, following closely the sequence of scenes in the Markan story. Later moves, however, invite the hearers to step back a bit from that plot and reflect on the implications of the story for the listeners.)

*Buttrick "moves":* A "move" within the homiletic of David Buttrick is the basic unit of a sermon plot involving one single meaning. Buttrick devotes fully one half of his *Homiletic* to move theory, yet the basic description is simple. Any move consists first of an opening and closing system using simple and direct sentences to articulate the single meaning. The single meaning then is expanded through both conceptual and imagistic language — Buttrick observes that the conceptual language will need to be imaged in some concrete way after perhaps four or five sentences. Other aspects of the move include contrapuntal statements and an insistence that every image provided by the preacher come equipped with a strong point of view. (See my *A New Hearing,* chap. 5, and Buttrick's *Homiletic,* pp. 23–170.)

At a third level of distance from the text are sermons in which an idea broadly based on something in the Bible is expounded or in which a certain situation in church or world is brought into the consideration of "Christian consciousness," or what Buttrick has called the mode of *praxis.* Buttrick describes this approach as preaching that "addresses persons in lived experience and, therefore, starts with a hermeneutic of lived experience" (*Homiletic*, p. 405). This praxis mode deals with questions of decision, stressing some general, practical implication of the Gospel.

An example of preaching in the mode of praxis is Joanna Adams's sermon "The Only Question," which appears in *A Chorus of Witnesses* (pp. 268-70). It is a funeral sermon preached in response to an intense situation involving a family murder/suicide. While the sermon does not deal specifically with one scriptural text, it relates the Gospel to the grievers and their situation with great solace.

Moving out further in homiletic space, we come to preaching that has completely broken out of its orbit around Scripture — the mode of *generic infection*. According to McClure, such a sermon has "no biblical text as part of the sermon preparation process, liturgy, or preaching itself" (*The Four Codes of Preaching*, pp. 18-19). Preaching this far removed from the Bible is already located within a homiletic pitfall of vast proportions — it has moved outside the most generous definitions of the genre of biblical preaching. It has become something else.

The danger here is that although such preaching may sound very Christian and may be very well motivated, at heart it has only a generic message to pass on to the audience. Preaching that descends into this particular pitfall faces several specific problems, involving hermeneutics, the question of authority, and the spiritual formation of the hearers.

### Hermeneutics

If hermeneutics considers how the church shall interpret its ancient scriptural texts for the contemporary situation, then at one level the generic infection mode of pulpit speech seems to simply bypass the issue. That is, because there is no particular biblical material present and accounted for in this "preaching," the "preacher" is relieved of most of the difficult questions of interpretation.

This strategy, however, really only pretends to avoid issues of interpretation (i.e., even in homiletics, "You can run but you can't hide"). Since all communication occurs within some interpretive context, the interesting question is what implicit hermeneutics lurks within the generic infection model. We are close to the target if we assume a position from within a model of doctrine that George Lindbeck terms the "experiential expressive." Within this model, Christian faith is authorized by some other worldview external to Scripture and Christian tradition; Christianity becomes only one example of the other worldview. This can be seen, for example, in some of the literature of the so-called men's movement, which addresses "the way things really are" through mythic stories culled from all sorts of cultures and religions — including, but not limited to, Christian faith (which is often viewed as having distorted the mythic foundations of male experience).

## Authority

It is hard to see that the generic infection model of preaching has much, if any, connection with a calling to the ministry of the Word. What authority, then, does preaching in this model possess? The experiential/expressive model of doctrine and the preacher who follows it must find their authority located in a worldview that shares some of the terms and personalities of Christian faith. The authority of such preaching may actually be located in the realm of self-help pop psychology, in the ideology underlying liberal political correctness, or perhaps in the New Age fascination with crystals, spirit lines, raised consciousness, and channeling. (I have listened to preaching that held each of these examples as the authority model for what was said.) In all of these instances, Jesus himself may be put forward as a great example — but only as he illustrates the values and vision of this other, non-Christian worldview.

## Spiritual Formation

We are formed as persons and as communities by the stories we share and the images that provide us with the means to envision ourselves and our world. Since persons do not inhabit neutral spaces without narratives or images, the issue becomes the truthfulness of these competing story traditions and their imagery. Let us make no mistake here: a church diminished in its biblical narrative and imagery will still be formed by stories, but it will be formed by those of the world. As Craig Dykstra has made clear, we can act only within a world we envision, and therefore our "worldly" formation will leave us Christian folk acting — and sounding — very much like the world. Lamentably, the generic infection approach to Scripture and preaching has rendered us particularly susceptible as a people to infection by the world's ideologies, images, and slogans. The pitfall here is preaching that is so distanced from the biblical story that the listeners hear only the stories of the world and thus lose a vision shaped by the Word.

### For further reading

Dykstra, Craig. *Vision and Character: A Christian Educator's Alternative to Kohlberg.* New York: Paulist Press, 1981.

Eslinger, Richard. *Narrative and Imagination: Preaching the Worlds That Shape Us.* Minneapolis: Fortress Press, 1995.

Lindbeck, George. *The Nature of Doctrine: Religion and Theology in a Postliberal Age.* Philadelphia: Westminster Press, 1984.

Long, Thomas G., and Cornelius Plantinga, Jr., eds. *A Chorus of Witnesses: Model Sermons for Today's Preacher.* Grand Rapids: Wm. B. Eerdmans Publishing Co., 1994.

Lowry, Eugene. *How to Preach a Parable: Designs for Narrative Sermons.* Nashville: Abingdon Press, 1989.

McClure, John. *The Four Codes of Preaching: Rhetorical Strategies.* Minneapolis: Fortress Press, 1991.

## 2.8. "The" Primary Virtue

In our ideologically superheated situation in the churches, one single virtue or doctrine is frequently taken as primary and overriding for interpreting Scripture and Christian faith. Thus we may see a book with a title like *Justice Church,* in which the virtue of justice is given a supreme, magisterial status. Or we could collect a whole library of works in which a particular version of the doctrine of substitutionary atonement is given a similar dominating status. Such a "primary virtue" approach is usually built upon a critique of other positions but pays little or no attention to its own defensibility.

From the perspective of the biblical narrative, the initial question is whether or not we may speak of *the* primary virtue in the first place. Every time the apostle Paul constructs one of his lists of virtues, we find it slightly varied from his other lists and composed of a number of virtues held together by the revelation of God in Christ. Since Scripture and Christian tradition do not yield any single, magisterial virtue, it may logically be inferred that any claimed overriding virtue is being imported from some other social and ideological system, perhaps from Marxism or good old-fashioned American individualism. We could adopt it as a rule that whenever a "primary virtue" ideology is being propounded, it will be necessary to look elsewhere than the Scriptures of Israel and the New Israel for its source and meaning. (The one obvious exception is Jesus' announcement of the priority of love in Mark 12:30-31 and parallels. However, in his familiar hymn to love in 1 Corinthians 13, the apostle Paul locates this primary virtue in a family with faith and hope.)

The pitfall for preaching here is obvious. One consequence is an increasingly boring redundancy in the use of the word from the pulpit. For the laity, this homiletic pitfall quickly becomes a cause for humorous banter, or worse. "Well, I wonder what the preacher is going to talk about this morning?" members might ask each other with faint enthusiasm, rolling their eyes. Another consequence is that such a preacher will also be scrimping mightily on the other virtues of Christian life and mission. So the "justice church" preacher may de-emphasize the virtue of forgiveness to the extent that it disappears from homiletic attention. Likewise, the preacher riding a wave of success-oriented personal improvement will focus on the virtue of positive thinking and in the process will very likely avoid the Christian virtues of humility and servanthood.

Truly biblical preaching, in contrast, will delight in the "dance of diversity" within the full virtues-system of Christian faith. Moreover, as preachers, we will continue that dance throughout the Christian year as the focus on one virtue or set of virtues interplays with others.

*Hint:* One exercise that may help broaden our homiletic virtues-system is taking inventory of the ecumenical lectionary's lessons for the season of Advent. Identify the virtues highlighted within the various narratives, prophecies, and epistle texts of the season and then compare the lists. Draw lines making connections between these virtues as the lessons convey them. Which virtues are at the center of the Advent celebration — a sense of awe, a passion for justice, humility, or perhaps patience? Now compare this Advent virtues-system with past sermons during the season. How do the two virtues-systems — the scriptural and the sermonic — relate? More and more frequently, preachers are coming together to study the Scriptures for the upcoming seasons. This exercise may be quite profitable for an entire lectionary study group as well.

## For further reading

Eslinger, Richard. *Narrative and Imagination: Preaching the Worlds That Shape Us,* chap. 1. Minneapolis: Fortress Press, 1995.

Hauerwas, Stanley. *A Community of Character: Toward a Constructive Christian Social Ethic.* Notre Dame, Ind.: University of Notre Dame Press, 1981.

Roberts, Robert C. "The Grammar of a Virtue." In *The Grammar of the Heart: Thinking with Kierkegaard and Wittgenstein,* ed. Richard H. Bell, pp. 149–70. San Francisco: Harper & Row, 1988.

## 2.9. Out of Praxis

*In preaching we do well to remember that the op-
posite of a God of love is not a God of anger but a
passive God.*

Paul Scott Wilson, "Beyond Narrative:
Imagination in the Sermon"

One of the contributions of Latin American liberation theology is
the distinctive notion of *praxis,* or practical action called for by the
Gospel. More specifically, liberationists insist that for the Word of
God in Scripture to be most keenly heard and appropriated, the
community of interpretation needs to be the poor of the earth or
those who have consciously made the decision to be in solidarity
with the poor. The hermeneutic key, liberation interpreters insist,
is that God sides with the poor. The hermeneutic circle, these
interpreters further argue, originates in the biblical narrative's witness to God's preferential option for the poor. The God of Israel
announces to the power of Pharaoh's Egypt a message of liberation
for those in bondage, which becomes the type of all of Scripture's
witness to liberation. As Walter Brueggemann has put it, the Bible
has a "vested interest" in the matter of liberation ("The Social
Nature of the Biblical Text for Preaching").

At the other side of the hermeneutic circle is our church situation, which exists in the midst of a world divided between the haves
and the have-nots. Those with eyes to see, however, notice that
systems of oppression oppress everyone, including those who presumably benefit most from the exercise of political, military,
economic, or churchly power. Within such a context, to act with
and on behalf of the dispossessed is to align ourselves with Israel's
narrative and with the purposes of God. Moreover, to align ourselves
with the poor is to discover the gospel truth about the first being
last and the last first. Liberation theology's notion of praxis involves
the conditions, actions, and commitments whereby we may interpret Scripture from the perspective insisted on by Scripture itself —
the underside, the side of the poor and the oppressed. Interpretation
lacking this essential commitment to praxis is not more objective

in its findings; rather, it is a distorted version of the faith that inevitably will serve the interests of entrenched power against the oppressed of the world. For this reason and others, modern liberalism is most frequently the position to come under attack by liberation theologians (see González and González, *The Liberating Pulpit,* pp. 24–26). Any position for interpretation that claims a neutral "objectivity" will most likely be a parochial perspective located within unrecognized privilege. To be lacking in praxis is a profound shortcoming when interpreting and preaching the biblical faith.

An equally vigorous attack on the dominant liberal approach to the interpretation of Scripture today is being mounted by the evangelical churches. While they and the liberationists disagree with each other on a number of issues, they are united in their insistence that there is no neutral site on which liberal interpreters may stand and from which they may interpret and preach. While evangelicals have not shown much interest in the term "praxis," they do share with the liberationists an insistence on action as a hermeneutic context for reading and preaching the Word. Consequently, we hear a remarkably parallel argument from evangelicals — namely, that Scripture intends a community engaged in specific evangelical activities, the foremost being that of bearing witness to the world about the Good News in Christ. The evangelical churches even employ a similar notion of the hermeneutic circle. To paraphrase Brueggemann, we can add that the New Testament Scriptures have a "vested interest" in the salvation of all persons through faith in Jesus Christ. From such a perspective, evangelical Christians would also call into question the wholeness of any interpretation of Scripture by individuals not involved in and committed to the evangelization of persons outside the community of faith.

At this point our previous reflections on the question about whether there is a single primary virtue again come to the forefront. Much of the argument between evangelicals and liberationists has grown out of the evangelical cry for "redemption" and the liberationist cry for "justice," as if Scripture presents these dominical imperatives as an either-or. In fact, there are other Christian communities and traditions whose construals of praxis are also to be considered and received. The Catholic tradition would insist that sacramental praxis be among the actions of the community interpreting the text of the day. Postliberal narrative theologians say that in addition to all of the above, the biblical virtue of hospitality is an essential element in Christian praxis, including a hospitality toward the biblical narrative itself. (See my *Narrative and Interpretation,* pp. 31–32.) Praxis here (with Stanley Hauerwas) would involve a nexus of activities and relationships within the church that would remind the world that it *is* the world and therefore in need of redemption.

All of these perspectives would agree that the Bible has a vested interest in a community of faith engaged in ministries embodying the ministry of Jesus Christ. They would also concur that impoverishment at the level of praxis is a profound distortion of biblical faith and consequently of a biblical theology of Christ, church, and world. To preach "out of praxis" is indeed to be caught in a serious pitfall.

## For further reading

Brueggemann, Walter. "The Social Nature of the Biblical Text for Preaching." In *Preaching as a Social Act: Theology and Practice,* ed. Art Van Seters, pp. 127–65. Nashville: Abingdon Press, 1988.

Eslinger, Richard. *Narrative and Imagination: Preaching the Worlds That Shape Us.* Minneapolis: Fortress Press, 1995.

González, Justo L., and Catherine G. González. *The Liberating Pulpit.* Nashville: Abingdon Press, 1994.

Hauerwas, Stanley. *A Community of Character: Toward a Constructive Christian Social Ethic.* Notre Dame, Ind.: University of Notre Dame Press, 1981.

Lints, Richard. *The Fabric of Theology: A Prolegomenon to Evangelical Theology.* Grand Rapids: Wm. B. Eerdmans Publishing Co., 1993.

Rowland, Christopher, and Mark Corner. *Liberating Exegesis: The Challenge of Liberation Theology to Biblical Studies.* Louisville, Ky.: Westminster/John Knox Press, 1989.

# 3. Method

**D**uring the past era of discursive preaching, methodology was mainly a question of how to organize the sermon's themes and subthemes. A variety of sermonic structures could be constructed out of the building blocks of the component "points" or propositions available to the preacher. Most familiar — to the point of caricature — was the old three points and a poem.

More recently, however, a variety of new methodologies have come into being, marked by mobility and shaped in many cases by the movement and structure of the scriptural text itself. Preachers deal in homiletic plots today and are alert to how their speech forms a sequence of meanings. Increasingly, we do not traffic in points and theme sentences. The new homiletics has come into a relatively mature stage, as far as its understanding of method is concerned. It involves a radical shift from previous models of an argumentation-based approach. By now it has become rather clear what the restraints and possibilities are in this new homiletic terrain. It can be mapped after all.

## 3.1. Parallel Plots

*The world of the Bible was different from our world.*

Raymond Bailey, *Hermeneutics for Preaching*

A typical response of seminarian preachers to the "then-now" her-meneutic question is to set up a sermon that runs two parallel plots — one keyed to the biblical text, and one to the contemporary situation. It perhaps could best be described as "a little bit of then, a little bit of now." Sketching this narrative strategy might produce the path in the figure below.

Telling a present-day story

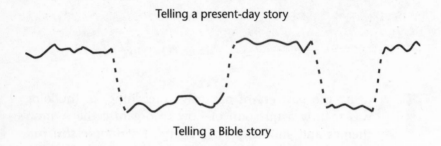

Telling a Bible story

A serious pitfall threatens this approach, no matter how carefully the plot lines are arranged in conjunction with one another. Notice that what we are asking the congregation to hear is one vast doublet system comprising frequent shifts in tense and points of view. Lamentably, as we have seen in section 1.5, doublets simply are not retained in congregational hearing, whether on the micro level (such as the phrase "peace and justice") or on the macro level of homiletic plot. One of the two plots may be retained by the hearers, most likely the one that displays the strongest imagery and atten-tion to character, setting, and immediacy of the issues (almost always the contemporary one). The other — usually the scriptural track — will fall out of communal awareness entirely. The doublet problem is compounded by the frequent shifts in tense that are built into the very method of the sermon itself. The hearers are the homiletic equivalent of spectators at a tennis match. They all look this way, and then that way, and then this way again. Tennis fans may be able to handle such a shift of attention, but the average congregation cannot sustain frequent changes in point of view. After two or three attempts to follow the shifts, the hearers will simply settle down within one or the other of the parallel plots.

58

The hermeneutic pitfall here is that a strategy of parallel align-ment of the biblical text and the contemporary world does not serve to integrate; ironically, it functions more to split the two apart. The formula in homiletic method — "alignment equals integration" — is unworkable in the real world of Sunday morning. Somehow, our methodology will need to reflect both our growing hermeneutic insights and our rhetorical savvy. Whatever method we adopt, (1) we will probably want to keep the homiletic plot in present tense; (2) we will provide the congregation with only one sequence of thought to follow, not two; and (3) only deliberately and with restraint will we shift congregational point of view.

> **Assignment:** Look at the stories of Jesus before Caiaphas and of Peter's denial in Matthew's Gospel (26:57-75). The narrative is "thick" with oppositions, character portrayals, turns of plot, and a tone of foreboding. What strategy would you adopt to retain these elements in a sermon on this text, at the same time avoiding the "parallel plots" pitfall as you strive for contem-poraneity? Write the sermon. Preach it.

## For further reading

Brown, Raymond E. *The Death of the Messiah: A Commentary on the Passion Narratives in the Four Gospels.* 2 vols. New York: Doubleday, 1994.

Eslinger, Richard. *Narrative and Imagination: Preaching the Worlds That Shape Us,* chap. 5. Minneapolis: Fortress Press, 1995. On methods of preaching.

Patte, Daniel. *The Gospel according to Matthew: A Structural Commentary on Matthew's Faith.* Philadelphia: Fortress Press, 1987.

## 3.2. Elephantine Intros

*Introductions require disciplined language.*

David Buttrick, *Homiletic*

For some reason, a trend has emerged over the last decade or so toward longer and longer sermon introductions. Perhaps this elongation of the introduction has to do with the breakdown in the modern paradigms of preaching and communication. That is, longer introductions may reflect an uneasiness with pulpit language and topical forms that we have inherited from the past. Or the dynamic may involve the growing insecurity about preaching — insecurity concerning ourselves, our authority, and perhaps even that of Scripture itself. Alternatively, these elephantine introductions may be serving as a plea for approval ("please like me, people . . . *please?*") or as an attempt to create congregational good feeling at the start of the sermon. For all of these reasons, and perhaps others, we are seeing an interesting evolution in the shape of the sermon. In some recorded cases, introductions have even dwarfed the body of the sermon itself!

The pitfalls involved in this elephantiasis of sermon introductions fall within three categories. First, long introductions make it harder for the hearers to get into the body of the sermon. The opening material may consist of several interwoven stories, perhaps with the intent of leading ultimately to some thematic point or other. If the stories are well told, the auditors may have trouble extricating themselves from these story-worlds and moving with the preacher into the main part of the sermon. Certainly, a good deal of sermonic material following extended anecdotal introductions will wind up being lost in the congregational hearing. Recognizing such a pitfall, we need to think rather of introductions as creating the readiness to hear the first move or other opening unit of the sermon itself. The introduction should increase, and not decrease, the capability of the hearers to receive the opening section of the sermon body.

A second pitfall concerns congregational attention. Expanding the introductory remarks of a sermon increases the likelihood that congregational attention will begin to wander. This restlessness is natural and in fact should be expected once the introduction moves beyond about twelve sentences in length. As the opening material expands beyond this threshold, in addition to the problem of wandering attention, there is the challenge of retrieving attention during the opening section of the sermon body. Often, it will take an especially well-done illustration in the sermon body to finally "bring them back." Furthermore, without any surrounding conceptual material to convey the meaning of opening illustrations, the hearers will attach their own meanings to the introduction. How much these coincide with the meanings intended by the preacher is open to debate.

A third pitfall related to these elongated introductions is that the material will begin to act as a sort of quasi-scriptural text. What will be exegeted and interpreted is the opening contemporary story-material, not the biblical narrative. Almost inevitably, the sermon begun by way of an extended anecdote will to some extent be shaped by the theological field implied in the opening story. The more extensive and detailed the opening story, the more likely it is to hold sway unduly over the following material in the sermon.

We are now in a good position to ask anew the purpose of a sermon introduction. How should it be constructed? The current options in homiletic method all assume that one purpose of the introduction is for the preacher to speak long enough for the hearers to be able to "tune in." Attentiveness to a public address does not begin instantaneously but typically takes at least three to five sentences. (This factor leads us to reject the old strategy of providing an opening theme sentence to the sermon. It seems that no one hears the opening sentence of oral communication in groups any longer!) The kind of speech needed as the congregation "dials in" is simple prose, with little in the way of compound or complex sentences. Moreover, these beginning sentences will offer an easy way for the congregation to consider the issues raised in the first section of the body of the sermon. Essentially, the introduction gathers congregational attention and then prepares it to hear what comes next.

While the purposes of an introduction will vary somewhat according to the homiletic method employed in the sermon, two functions are now to be considered "null and void." First, the introduction no longer needs to prepare the congregation to hear the entire sermon. We need only provide our hearers with a readiness to hear the first scene, move, or location of single meaning. Second, the introduction does not need to function as an interest builder. (Saying that it does seems to imply that the body of the sermon is necessarily boring!) In every method appropriate to this postmodern age, we will sustain interest throughout the sermon, utilizing the immediacy of imagery and the mobility of the homiletical plot.

*Assignment:* The specifications for a sermon utilizing the "Lowry Loop" mostly relate to an adequate portrayal of the bind or trouble implied in the biblical text. Read Lowry's *The Homiletic Plot,* pp. 22–73, as well as chapter 3 (on Lowry) in my *A New Hearing.* Then design opening systems for the following Scripture lessons:

Joel 2:12-17

Ephesians 5:15-20

Mark 10:35-45

*For further reading*

Buttrick, David. *Homiletic: Moves and Structures,* pp. 83–96. Philadelphia: Fortress Press, 1987.

Eslinger, Richard. *A New Hearing: Living Options in Homiletic Method.* chap. 5. Nashville: Abingdon Press, 1987.

Long, Thomas G. *The Witness of Preaching,* pp. 133–47. Louisville, Ky.: Westminster/John Knox Press, 1989.

Lowry, Eugene. *The Homiletical Plot: The Sermon as Narrative Art Form,* pp. 22–35. Atlanta: John Knox Press, 1980.

Wilson, Paul Scott. *The Practice of Preaching,* pp. 182–84. Nashville: Abingdon Press, 1995.

## 3.3. The Sermon as Essay

One of the complaints heard from novices about the sermon-writing routine is that it takes so long. In many cases, this comment is really an admission that the neophyte preacher doesn't have a clue as to sermon methodology. For the novice, the task of sermon writing may be essentially to write an essay each week, starting every Monday morning with a completely blank computer screen. Ironically, our essayist may have had extensive training in seminary in the craft of historical-critical exegesis. What to do sermonically with all that detail, however, remains obscure. So almost every week, there is the same quandary of how to write a pastorally appropriate sermon related to all this fine exegesis. "Another week, another essay," goes the lament. The discontinuity between biblical interpretation and homiletic method is the problem and the pitfall.

At the outset, we should note that the sermon as essay will create difficulties in communication simply because of its literary style. Preachers need to realize that oral rhetoric is a different use of language than literary writing. Neither can be substituted for the other. Hence, the essay model of the sermon is already flirting with a pitfall simply at the level of communal rhetoric. Put simply, a literary style is not the language of preaching. Moreover, the essay model will almost invariably bias the preacher toward an idea-centered redaction of the biblical text, what we have labeled "slow-cooking" the text (see sec. 2.2 above). Some isolated idea found to lurk within the pericope is then extracted and expounded on at length in the essay-sermon.

It is probably more common today for preachers to be in search of a homiletic method than it was in the good old days of three points and a poem. At least during the reign of the old discursive homiletic, almost everyone shared general assumptions as to sermon method and sermon shape. Now, in the wake of the collapse of this rationalist paradigm, the preacher may know how he or she will *not* organize a sermon — but what methodology will take its place? The good news, however, is that we are now into our second decade of the new homiletics. From this vantage point we may observe that the viable options in homiletic method all share several traits in common. Here we consider three of them.

## *Merging of Exegesis and Homiletics*

There is no longer a sharp dichotomy between biblical exegesis and homiletic method. Rarely do we now hear encouragement to complete the work of scriptural interpretation before beginning the task of sermon-making. Rather, the preacher/interpreter is urged to be thinking homiletic strategy even while he or she is engaged in interpretation. The movement and structure of a biblical text is now of keen interest to the preacher, since, in many cases, it will be reflected directly in the moves of the sermon. In other cases, the issues or questions found within the pericope will become the "torque" (Lowry's term) around which the homiletic plot takes form. In contrast, an exegetical process that "breaks open" some biblical text (read "verse") to discover some thematic or main idea that is subsequently developed homiletically is not favored by most recent biblical studies and approaches to preaching.

## *Episodes, Not Points*

Unlike the essay model, with its relatively seamless and free-flowing development, most homiletic methods sharing a postcritical perspective are episodic in some way or other. A sermon that operates with an immediacy to the biblical text will have an internal organization in which its episodes are shaped by the "scenes" or "moves" of the text. (One reason for the attention to preaching parables is that they yield most directly a sequence of scenes that may become the components of the homiletic plot.) In fact, a new language is being developed by biblical interpreters and homileticians to speak of these surface-level episodes in Scripture and in preaching — "moves," "lexies," and "stages" are three of the labels given to these sermon components. Whatever our method, we are more likely to be forming a plot composed of these episodes than we are to be assembling points, themes, and subthemes.

## Sermonic Sequence

For language to be retained in the act of oral communication within a group, it must be designed in the congregational hearing as relatively brief components-in-sequence. These components (e.g., the moves) will all have a relationship to each other that the preacher shapes from the start of the sermon-writing process. Rather than beginning with a blank computer screen, the preacher may more helpfully have a worksheet or chart related to one specific sermon method, on which are entered the scenes of the biblical text and ideas on sermonic moves that develop the scenes. These sermons will differ in specifics; all, however, will be episodic and inherently mobile, reflecting some notion of a homiletic plot.

*Assignment:* Because of their straightforward structure and movement, parables are one of the easiest types of biblical literature in which to identify possible homiletic plots. With the assistance of Pheme Perkins, Bernard Brandon Scott, and others, analyze the parable of the rich man and Lazarus (Luke 16:19-31) in terms of its scenes, or lexies. Next, propose a sermonic "move" for some or all of the scenes in the text. Finally, determine the best sequence of moves for presentation in a sermon.

Did you use all the parable's scenes, or only certain ones? What about the sequence of the sermonic moves? Will the sequence match that of the parable, or is there reason to shift their order?

*For further reading*

Bartlett, David L. "Texts Shaping Sermons." In *Listening to the Word: Studies in Honor of Fred B. Craddock,* ed. Gail R. O'Day and Thomas G. Long, pp. 147–63. Nashville: Abingdon Press, 1993.

Buttrick, David. *A Captive Voice: The Liberation of Preaching,* pp. 91–99. Louisville, Ky.: Westminster/John Knox Press, 1994. Buttrick's reading of the Rich Man and Lazarus.

Donahue, John R. *The Gospel in Parable,* pp. 169–72. Philadelphia: Fortress Press, 1988.

Long, Thomas G. *Preaching and the Literary Forms of the Bible.* Philadelphia: Fortress Press, 1988.

Perkins, Pheme. *Hearing the Parables of Jesus,* pp. 67–72. New York: Paulist Press, 1981.

Scott, Bernard Brandon. *Hear Then the Parable: A Commentary on the Parables of Jesus,* pp. 141–59. Minneapolis: Fortress Press, 1989.

## 3.4. Storytelling Misfires

*Illustrations often assume a life of their own, and neither the preacher nor the congregation can remember what they were illustrations of.*

Richard Lischer, "Preaching
as the Church's Language"

While interpretive pitfalls bedevil preaching-as-storytelling, those who intend to "preach the story" also encounter a variety of other pitfalls — what I here call storytelling misfires. These mostly stem from the power of a story to draw listeners into the "world" of the story. The more effective the storytelling, the more likely it is that the hearers will remain lodged there, unable to move on with the preacher to the rest of the sermon. A "homeostasis principle" is at work in the community hearing of a well-told story. Unless care is taken to "move" the audience out of that environment, they will tend to remain right there. Several pitfalls relate directly to this principle of narrative homeostasis.

## *Imbalance*

Any story the preacher begins that evokes strong listener memories runs the risk of growing out of control, thus throwing the sermon as a whole out of balance. This pitfall is present whenever the sermon contains a modern-day story that illustrates or follows the text.

One approach to narrative is Eugene Lowry's "running the story" approach, in which the plot of the sermon matches the narrative plot of the scriptural text. If, for example, the text is the Great Flood narrative of Genesis 7–8, an obvious tactic for preachers whose churches had experienced the "great flood" of the Mississippi River in 1993 would be to relate images and stories from that powerful event to the biblical story. Assume that a church had been saved from the rising waters by the efforts of many townspeople, aided by volunteers from the state prison work farm. We can easily imagine our preacher portraying the parallels between Noah's work on the ark in the face of the rising flood and the work on the levee around the church. A rather terse reference in the sermon to recent events may well establish a powerful analogy between the feverish work on the ark and on the efforts on the dam around the church.

We would encounter a problem, though, if the preacher spent a good deal of time and descriptive effort elaborating on the recent flooding, adding stories within stories about this recent event. Consider how the following comments would affect the overall balance of the sermon:

> *John Wayman, remember, he brought his 'dozer up here from the farm and scraped up the pile of dirt for us to use in making all those sandbags . . . remember the noise that old "cat" made. . . . John, have you bought a new one yet? . . . And remember how those prisoners from the state farm worked right there beside us . . . why you'd think it was their church they were trying to save . . . and right there was the start of our prison ministry, . . . a wonderful outreach by our Social Concerns Committee.*

The obvious pitfall here is that with such immediacy of detail invoking congregational memories, it will be almost impossible for the preacher to float back to Noah and his challenges with the congregation tagging along. The contemporary story has become too extended and dominant in building an imagined (and in this case remembered) world for the congregation. It ceases to function as an example story or analogy and becomes the narrative home of the hearers. Any subsequent dealing with Noah will most likely be peripheral to this now-dominant story of the recent flood. A related problem is that the contemporary story has introduced material not all that congruent with the biblical story. For example, we may need to postpone references to the prison work teams and the new prison ministry until a more fitting place in another sermon.

## Overpowering Style

Another pitfall related to homeostasis in story sermons concerns the easily overpowering nature of the narrative rhetorical style. The preacher may desire to use a story or story-portion taken from contemporary literature as the sermonic plot. Let's say, for example, that a preacher selects large portions of Annie Dillard's *Pilgrim at Tinker Creek* as the body of the storytelling sermon. Perhaps the subject is Dillard's powerful description of the moth and the flame along with her feelings and reflections. Occasionally, the preacher may interrupt the Dillard story to inject comments that attempt to connect explicitly with some aspect of the local church situation.

Given these choices of our preacher, however, two outcomes are almost guaranteed. First, the Dillard material, with its power of description, will be strongly retained in the congregational hearing; little will be lost regarding the moth and the flame. Second, any relationship between the meanings the hearers draw from the story and those the preacher wanted them to draw will be random at best. Appending some comments related to the "message" of a powerful story told from the pulpit will do little to ensure that the congregation really grasps the meanings intended.

## Overpowering Introductions

The use of an extended story as the sermon introduction has recently become rather prevalent (see sec. 3.2). The homeostasis principle with regard to preached narrative, however, makes it clear that the congregation will tend to have difficulty extricating itself from these opener stories and moving on with the sermon. Typically, the hearers will sit tight in the story's setting until explicitly "relocated" by the preacher.

The old homiletic theory assumed that enumeration will function as a story stopper. Unfortunately, enumeration no longer serves to evoke much, if any, effect in a congregation's hearing; an enumerated point will not extricate the congregation from a vast story introduction. The congregation won't budge from a powerful introduction just because the people hear from the pulpit, "We now turn to our first point."

## First-Person Dangers

The use of first-person stories in sermons, which has now become common, is rife with pitfalls. In such sermons, the preacher tells a lengthy personal story in the first person, sometimes as an introduction or illustration, but occasionally as the sermon in its entirety. We have already considered the general problem of moving a congregation on, once it has settled into the world of a story. This challenge also exists in the first-person story sermon, but there are other severe problems as well that are distinctive to this genre of narrative.

One pitfall is the tendency of the congregation to look for connections between the "I" sermon and the current relation between preacher and congregation. For example, a reference in the sermon to the preacher's serious illness as a teenager may well evoke concerns as to the preacher's present health. ("The 'Rev.' really didn't look too well the other night at the board meeting, did he?" the hearer might ponder.) First-person stories from the pulpit are notorious in their tendency to spawn attendant pastor-parish concerns. (For additional issues, see sec. 4.4 on first-person illustrations.)

Our primary focus at this point, however, is on the full first-person anecdotal sermon. "Powerful" is probably too weak a word for this method. The story will in almost every instance form in congregational hearing — and likely be remembered for years. Also retained will be the attendant musings of the hearers evoked by first-person pulpit references. For better or worse, the preacher has little or no control over the dynamics of these musings.

> *Hint:* We all have to contend with narrative homeostasis in our preaching. We can help hearers come to closure on a story, though, by giving attention to the sense of an ending, by letting everyone know that the story has indeed stopped. Check out David Buttrick's suggestions on closure systems as a way of locating the narrative within the single meaning you intend (*Homiletic,* pp. 50–53). Also see chapter 5 in my *Narrative and Imagination.*

### For further reading

Buttrick, David. *Homiletic: Moves and Structures.* Philadelphia: Fortress Press, 1987.

Eslinger, Richard. *Narrative and Imagination: Preaching the Worlds That Shape Us.* Minneapolis: Fortress Press, 1995.

Dillard, Annie. *Pilgrim at Tinker Creek.* New York: Harper & Row, 1974.

## 3.5. Runaway Ideas

One of the perennial problems related to the old topical preaching was keeping the points all separate and distinct. When a new point was enumerated, hearers might often respond, "Five? I thought we were on three!" Points seemed to drop out of congregational awareness as easily as overripe fruit does from a tree. While a good deal of the problem had to do with the rhetoric of discursive preaching, other factors contributed as well.

A notable pitfall relates to a lack of attention to closure systems, both within the "three points" approach and within more recent homiletic methods. If the community is attending to a single meaning at some location within the sermon, and if that meaning is well imaged, simply announcing the number or the topic of the next section will not be enough to close the hearers' participation in the prior location. Even rather clear signals that a new meaning is being developed may not serve to close off attention to the previous location's meaning. Somewhat ironically, this pitfall increases in its likelihood in relation to the relative power of the prior meaning for the congregation. In other words, a well-developed move or homiletic location, with strong imagery and point of view, will build a "world" within which the hearers will find a place. Simply beginning a new thought will not dislodge the "inhabitants" of that world. We will need to deliberately close off participation in that sermonic location.

The pitfall of not closing down runaway ideas occurs predictably in the following scenarios:

— A strongly developed move or other type of single meaning in the sermon. The congregation will likely have trouble dislocating itself from that meaning or move; simply beginning a new conceptual element will not necessarily move the hearers along.

— A point or other section of a sermon that is concluded with a strong narrative illustration. Again, the congregation will find itself within the narrative world of the illustration and will not be easily dislodged.

— A narrative sermon based on a biblical story in which the preacher attempts to make an excursus in order to contemporize the implications at stake. (Lowry labels this method "running the story"; see his *How to Preach a Parable*, pp. 42–78.) Simply saying, "Even in our own day, we find . . . ," or words to that effect, will not serve to dislodge the hearers from reflecting on the biblical narrative.

— A first-person story told by the preacher that involves considerable affective power. Here, even a well-developed closure system may not be enough to extricate the hearers from remaining in that place of pathos.

One way to find out whether the hearers were able to move on with ease to the next place in the sermon is simply to ask them. That is, recruit a small group of debriefers who will meet with you sometime after the worship service (and any fellowship hour!). Begin each session with the question, "How did I begin?" and "Where did we go then?" If large chunks of material in the sermon have disappeared from the awareness of your hearers, one possible explanation is that a story or idea has been developed quite effectively but then was not closed off well. Now the issue becomes, What's a preacher to do?

The easiest method for closing off a location of single meaning within a sermon is by reiteration. The preacher simply shifts to a simpler rhetoric, restates the single meaning in two or three sentences, and pauses. Such a pause is rather important, for it gives time for the communal consciousness to do its own closure workings.

A Buttrick "move" will be formed with both opening and closing systems very much in mind. In fact, a single meaning is not really a move until a closure system has been added to the interconnected conceptual language and imagery. (See Buttrick, *Homiletic,* pp. 50–53.)

Within a narrative sermon that runs the story, the challenge is often that the narrative must be put on hold while an excursus into contemporary reflection is developed. Say, for example, a narrative sermon is developing the story of Jonah and the preacher wants to put the plot on hold and expand on the issue of running away from God in the contemporary situation. First, a few reiterative statements are made, such as, *"So there's Jonah, out on that boat, running away from the Lord, seeking political asylum from the will of God."* Then the following excursus can begin: *"Think that sort of folly was just in Old Testament times? . . . that old Jonah was the only one to try to flee away from God's will? 'Not on your life,' Jonah would say to us, 'not on your life.' Look, here we are, secure out here from most of those awful problems of the inner city, and. . . ."*

Another methodological strategy when preaching a narrative

sermon is to contemporize the story all along. In this case, the narrative does not need much in the way of pauses. Rather, we might just pick up after the lot fell to Jonah with a segue that begins, *"Now I don't know about you, but I'm sure glad that dice roll went to Jonah. Aren't you, shipmates . . . ?"*

---

*Assignment:* One of the finest examples of a contemporary re-telling of the story of Noah is by Dennis M. Willis in Eugene Lowry's *How to Preach a Parable* (the book's title reflects only a partial expression of the full sweep of this fine work). As you read Willis's sermon "Noah Was a Good Man" (pp. 42–49), list the ways in which description and dialogue serve to contemporize the biblical story. Note the way Willis brings closure to the parts of his sermon.

---

*For further reading*

Buttrick, David. *Homiletic: Moves and Structures.* Philadelphia: Fortress Press, 1987.

Lowry, Eugene. *How to Preach a Parable: Designs for Narrative Sermons.* Nashville: Abingdon Press, 1989.

## 3.6. Doing Space

*A sermon is an ordered form of moving time.*

Eugene Lowry, *Doing Time in the Pulpit*

"Most of us," Eugene Lowry remarks, "were trained to think space and not time" (*Doing Time in the Pulpit,* p. 12). That is, our education and formation as preachers was mostly centered on the spatial image of concepts, of propositions and main ideas. This dominant

image informed our approach to the interpretation of Scripture —
we hunted down the "main ideas" of the parables and searched out
the "message" of most any text. Then, as we preachers turned to
the task of sermon preparation, the spatial image became articulated
through terms from various building trades. We read about the *craft*
of sermon construction (as in W. E. Sangster's text *The Craft of
Sermon Illustration*), and we *built* sermons composed of points and
subpoints. While we have critiqued the hermeneutic aspects of this
spatial and rationalistic model (see Pitfalls 2.2 and 2.3), its implications for sermon methodology are similarly flawed. In Lowry's
terms, the methodological pitfall is that of doing space rather than
time in the pulpit.

A spatially conceived sermon has as its rhetorical foundation the
Hellenistic model of argumentation. The goal of this discursive,
spatially shaped speech is that of persuasion. As Don Wardlaw
observes, "Preaching, per se, has meant marshalling an argument
in logical sequence, coordinating and subordinating points by the
canons of logic, all in a careful appeal to the reasonable hearer"
(*Preaching Biblically*, p. 12). Certainly we must admit that the spatial
model of preaching did introduce temporality into the outlined
argument in the way of illustrations utilizing narrative, metaphor,
and imagery. Yet it must also be acknowledged that these expressions of mobility were located securely within a spatially structured
sermon. "Narration itself is allowed to work only within the carefully defined limits of the anecdote, the historical allusion, or the
illustration enlisted to make a point or win an argument" (*Preaching
Biblically*, p. 13). Wardlaw adds that the occasional exceptions to
the discursive model — such as dramatic sermons and first-person
monologues — only serve to prove the rule; they are clearly exceptions to the reigning model of discursive preaching.

The trouble is that the old model no longer serves the church
well. Its "distillation" approach to the meaning of Scripture can
no longer be sustained, its conceptual language no longer functions very well rhetorically, and its methodology of assembling
ideas into points and propositions has become almost impossible
for hearers to follow. The spatial model is well along the road
to obsolescence. The alternative — "doing time" — involves a
thoroughgoing transformation of the preaching task. Lowry has

74

charted the alternatives of spatial and temporally based preaching as in the figure below.

| The Ordering of | | |
|:---:|:---:|:---:|
| *IDEAS* | | *EXPERIENCE* |
| **The** | | |
| ORGANIZE | TASK | SHAPE |
| STRUCTURE | FORM | PROCESS |
| THEME | FOCUS | EVENTS |
| SUBSTANCE | PRINCIPLE | RESOLUTION |
| OUTLINE | PRODUCT | PLOT |
| LOGIC/CLARITY | MEANS | AMBIGUITY/SUSPENSE |
| UNDERSTANDING | GOAL | HAPPENING |

Eugene L. Lowry, *Doing Time in the Pulpit*, p. 27.

At stake in the pitfall of doing space is the methodological issue rather than the interpretive one. It may seem that we are asking solely the homiletic question of a sermon's movement and structure, and not the antecedent question of the narrative dynamics of the text. However, this is not the case. Inevitably, in preaching based on a story in Scripture that "does time," the text's plot and intention shape the sermon. Different methods of doing time are available to us, however, all of which faithfully bring the narrative text to a new hearing.

The difference between the two models is best grasped with reference to preaching based on a specific biblical narrative. Consider, for example, the story of the command to Abraham to sacrifice Isaac in Genesis 22. Two examples of sermons on this story are readily available for study and comparison: John Holbert's sermon "The Best Laugh of All," in his book *Preaching Old Testament* (pp. 79–84), and David Buttrick's sermon "Abraham and Isaac," in my *A New Hearing* (pp. 166–69). The former is "pure narrative" (Holbert's phrase), while the latter is based on Buttrick's method of moves and structures. As a means of sharpening the distinctions between the two approaches, compare the sermons with reference to the following questions:

— What scenes does Holbert develop in his sermon? What moves does Buttrick make? What sequence does each follow? (That is, what is the homiletic plot of each?) Compare the two plots for momentum and ease of following. (Buttrick understands a sermon to comprise a series of moves, each developing a conceptual component, yet all related in an easy-to-follow series of thoughts. Holbert's narrative approach may appear more "seamless" in its retelling of the biblical story. Even in a "pure narrative" sermon, however, an internal structuring of the plot will be evident as a series of scenes in succession.)

— How does each preacher speak about and image Abraham's obedience? Is clear and vivid imagery provided here? Compare.

— How does Holbert's narrative sermon achieve (or fail to achieve) the essential task of contemporizing the text in the hearing of the congregation? How does Buttrick's sermon fare with the same question? (Both methodologies intend the text to be contemporized in the hearing of the congregation. Notice that Buttrick devotes an entire concluding move to the task of making the message contemporary.)

— How do the two sermons differ in their introductions and conclusions? What differences do you see in length, kind of language employed, and point of view? (With different methods, the question is not which preacher does better than the other. Rather, how effective are the beginnings and endings relative to the specific method of each sermon?)

*For further reading*

Eslinger, Richard. *A New Hearing: Living Options in Homiletic Method.* Nashville: Abingdon Press, 1987.

Holbert, John C. *Preaching Old Testament: Proclamation and Narrative in the Hebrew Bible.* Nashville: Abingdon Press, 1991.

Lowry, Eugene. *Doing Time in the Pulpit: The Relationship between Narrative and Preaching.* Nashville: Abingdon Press, 1985.

Wardlaw, Don M., ed. *Preaching Biblically: Creating Sermons in the Shape of Scripture.* Philadelphia: Westminster Press, 1983.

## 3.7. Sermon Nuggets

In certain preaching traditions, sermons are construed as growing from germinated ideas. In the age of the "pulpit giants," such sermon ideas were encapsulated into the titles themselves. (In a 1927 book of sermons entitled *If I Had Only One Sermon to Preach: Sermons by Twenty-one Ministers,* titles included "The Triune Entirety of the Christian Revelation," "The Curse of Cynicism," and "Incontestable Fact and Indispensable Truth.") Although we are living and preaching some fifty years after the end of that romantic pulpit age, still the practice continues. Along with the practice comes an implied notion of the sermon as feat or performance. Specifically, this practice assumes that the preacher may collect some quotation, poem, sermon title, or other "nugget" and, by virtue of its clever or novel content, build a sermon around it. Two preachers driving down the road together may glance at a church signboard as they go by. Reading the sermon title for the coming Sunday, one of them announces, "Hey, I could preach a sermon on that!" Our two preachers are about to drive into a preaching pothole — that of prospecting for sermon nuggets.

At the outset, let's admit that a biblical sermon may in fact have its origins in the snaring of some clever sermon idea. In order to avoid the sermon-nugget pitfall, however, the preacher-collector must be savvy enough immediately to locate that snared nugget within some specific text of Scripture. Otherwise, with little or no theological and homiletic control from a biblical pericope, the ensuing sermon will all too likely reflect the preacher's own biases and particular ideological orientation.

Even when a biblical text is located with reference to the nugget, a danger remains. As Elizabeth Achtemeier has observed, "The illustrative material will impose a meaning on the text which is not properly there and therefore may lead us to ignore the text in order to preserve the use of the illustration" (*Creative Preaching*, p. 116). The question, then, for those immersed in traditions that value sermon ideas is not strictly, Which comes first, the sermon idea nugget or the biblical text? The more fundamental issue relates to the primary context out of which the sermon grows. What factors give the sermon its primary movement, shape, and intention — the nugget itself, or the text that the nugget is illustrating?

A related pitfall inherent in sermon-nugget preaching is that with so little to go on — only a sermon title, poem fragment, or borrowed illustration — we will fall back into a discursive style of pulpit talk. Our sermon may contain largely "talk about" this nifty sermon nugget we have collected. Furthermore, we are likely to find ourselves "doing space" in the pulpit rather than "doing time" — that is, assembling static ideas rather than shaping mobile plots (see the previous pitfall, "Doing Space").

Finally, we should be aware (and also beware!) that our hobby of sermon-nugget collection is a very popular one. It is therefore likely that a good percentage of congregations have heard nugget-type preaching before. The desired virtue here of homiletic novelty is considerably compromised when the congregation has already heard our most recently gleaned sermon nugget. Suddenly, novelty is replaced by recognition, if not boredom.

*Assignment:* A growing literature in homiletics is devoted to the discipline of shaping sermons more fully according to the scriptural text. One particularly formative book is *Preaching Biblically,* edited by Don M. Wardlaw. Analyze the five sermon examples contained in the book and notice how the formative principle is more that of plot than theme sentence or single germinating idea.

For a thoughtful reconsideration of the role of the concept in preaching, see David Greenhaw, "As One with Authority: Rehabilitating Concepts in Preaching," in *Intersections: Post-Critical Studies in Preaching,* ed. Richard Eslinger (Grand Rapids: Wm. B. Eerdmans Publishing Co., 1994), pp. 105–22. Also consider Paul Scott Wilson's presentation of a somewhat rehabilitated notion of the "point" in preaching in his *Practice of Preaching,* pp. 205–19. Contrast Wilson's retrieval of the sermonic point with Lowry's critique in *Doing Time in the Pulpit.*

## For further reading

Achtemeier, Elizabeth. *Creative Preaching: Finding the Words*. Nashville: Abingdon Press, 1980.

Keck, Leander E. *The Bible in the Pulpit: The Renewal of Biblical Preaching*. Nashville: Abingdon Press, 1978.

Lowry, Eugene. *Doing Time in the Pulpit: The Relationship between Narrative and Preaching*. Nashville: Abingdon Press, 1985.

Wardlaw, Don M., ed. *Preaching Biblically: Creating Sermons in the Shape of Scripture*. Philadelphia: Westminster Press, 1983.

Wilson, Paul Scott. *The Practice of Preaching*, pp. 182–84. Nashville: Abingdon Press, 1995.

## 3.8. And in Conclusion

Perhaps no component of the sermon is fraught with more pitfalls than the conclusion. Indeed, confusion about conclusions may be symptomatic of the more general problems concerning preaching these days. Take, for instance, the rather obvious affirmation that a sermon's conclusion ought to conclude the sermon. Most everyone who regularly attends Sunday worship can spot the oddly disrupting homily that has no sense of an ending whatever — when it feels like the preacher simply has run out of words to read on his or her manuscript and sits down. Having heard sermons that really don't have any concluding material and having been left in the air by such preaching, we are ready to conclude that conclusions need to conclude!

The problems do not disappear, however, merely by making our conclusions conclude. An equally problematic tendency is to pack too much into the sermon's conclusion. This pitfall typically occurs through a strategy of reiteration, beginning with phrases such as, "And now in conclusion . . ." or "Finally, let us now conclude. . . ." With the congregation thereby signaled that a conclusion is underway, attention is now turned to other things and away from the conclusion's content. Moreover, the tendency to overconclude ("And in conclusion, let us first recall that . . .") actually reduces rather than reinforces motivation. Things are tied together too neatly, too perfectly begun and ended. The congregational attention and intentionality are both significantly reduced.

Let's consider several other pitfalls that regularly afflict sermon conclusions.

### Reiteration

One common temptation is to restate themes or points by a system of ordered repetition in the conclusion. *("We must love, my dear friends, the neighbor who is nearby. We must love the neighbor who is far away. We must even love the neighbor who does not love in return.")* Facing such reiteration, the hearers are likely to drop entirely any engagement they might have had with the whole conclusion.

### Introducing a New Voice

Another detracting tendency in conclusions is to introduce a new sermonic voice. David Buttrick notes that such quotations shift point of view in the conclusion, which has a detrimental effect on the listeners. By way of such quoting, Buttrick adds, "the preacher will turn into a ventriloquist's dummy, looking straight at the congregation but speaking someone else's words; the effect on a congregation can be unnerving. The congregation will have to break with the speaker in order to adjust to someone else's syntax and to another voice speaking. Congregations do not return to the conclusion following a quote, but drift off into disengagement" (*Homiletic*, p. 104).

### Ending with a Question

The practice of ending a conclusion with a question has emerged in modern practice perhaps as an effort to make a prophetic gesture toward Christian commitment. Unfortunately, what actually occurs in sermons with a question as the tag line *("And so it once more is asked of all of us, will you or will you not take up your cross and follow Jesus?")* is that the question simply deletes from the congregational consciousness. While a sense of questioning reflectivity in many cases can and should permeate the conclusion, we will not want to end the sermon with an actual question. (See also sec. 1.9 above.)

### Mismatch in Affective States

A further pitfall is a conclusion that involves intensified preacherly affect. It is one of the mysteries of preaching these days that there is no necessary connection between the internal affective state of the preacher and that of the congregation. With the intention of evoking a strong affective state in hearers, the preacher may grab for a large, emotive anecdote; or he or she may break into a repetitive series of sentences. In the former case, the congregation might well

81

**Buttrick on conclusions** (all from his *Homiletic*):

*Conclusions are governed by intention.* At the same time, let us pin down the obvious: *Conclusions are designed to conclude* (p. 97).

One of the tasks of a conclusion is to establish a stopped reflective consciousness in the congregation (p. 101).

The sense of an ending is usually achieved by syntax, rhythmics, or by sounds of words (p. 103).

Conclusions ought to be concrete (p. 106).

Conclusions ought to be said in simple language (p. 107).

Conclusions do two things: they fulfill intention and they end (p. 108).

be lured into the pathos of the concluding story, but all too easily the people will tend to attach meanings not intended by the preacher. In the latter instance, the series of repetitive sentences may evoke a certain affect within the preacher but likely will not function in the same manner for the congregation. Most regularly, Buttrick observes, the repetitive system will not stick with the people, for "the minister will feel much and the congregation hear nothing" (*Homiletic,* p. 106).

## Undue Complexity

A final pitfall is a conclusion that contains complex internal organization and numerous shifts in point of view. This pitfall tends to undermine the function of a conclusion, which is not only to end the sermon but also to invite the hearers to adopt a certain unitary perspective regarding the intention of the sermon's plot.

For example, consider a sermon utilizing a narrative method based quite tightly on the plot of Luke 24:13-35, "The Walk to Emmaus." A conclusion of undue complexity might first quote some of the prophecies about Christ in the Old Testament, shift to a poem about the Lord's Supper, and end with a plea for the doctrine of the Real Presence of Christ in the Eucharist. Each of these parts of the conclusion involves a different voice as well as a shift in sermonic point of view. This conclusion will most likely boggle the congregation's mind; little if any of its content will form in the people's consciousness.

In contrast, noticing that the pericope has a quite specific intention toward recognizing the crucified and risen Lord as present when the church gathers and breaks bread, we might shape a conclusion as follows:

*So here we are, gathered together on this first day of the week. We've brought with us all those hopes and all that disappointment . . . brought them along with our bread and wine. And soon they will be offered, all of them, offered to our God and set here on the Table. Will it be just more bread of affliction, you think, . . . more cups of sorrow? Perhaps. But what if our Lord takes this bread and gives thanks and breaks it for us? Look at the transformation. Cup of joy, bread of heaven, . . . presence of the Lord. Come to the banquet; Christ is risen.*

## For further reading

Buttrick, David. *Homiletic: Moves and Structures,* pp. 100–109. Philadelphia: Fortress Press, 1987.

Long, Thomas G. *The Witness of Preaching,* pp. 150–55. Louisville, Ky.: Westminster/John Knox Press, 1989.

Wilson, Paul Scott. *The Practice of Preaching,* pp. 184–86. Nashville: Abingdon Press, 1995.

# 4. Illustration

Within both literature and public speech, imagination has been viewed as bringing near that which is far off. One purpose of illustration in the older homiletics was to effect that "bringing near" with immediacy and with purpose. The intent was to illustrate some idea, some conceptual point or proposition, thereby "hammering it home" in the awareness of the hearers. Preachers in earlier times mostly were aware that their rationalistic sermon structures were incapable of reaching the emotions of the hearers. Especially for those lacking in sophistication, the argument went, the illustration's purpose was to add a dimension of affect to the rational plea of the sermon. Stories — mostly they were anecdotal narratives — were the place where the point came home, moved the hearers, and retained their interest.

In the new homiletics we still write and talk about illustrations. The meaning of that term, though, has subtly shifted in homiletic discourse. (We almost need a new word to describe the new functioning.) For one thing, a more diverse repertoire of illustration is being encouraged than simply the anecdotal story. Moreover, the function of illustration is inevitably reoriented when the move is made from a rationalist to a narrative-based homiletic. No longer is the illustration construed as making some thematic point both tangible and vivid. Now, the illustration is seen more as the imagery around which conceptual sermonic material can gather in order for the entire spoken unit to form in the consciousness of the hearers. Put simply, the illustration now works as the essential "speck" around which the conceptual ice crystals grow to form the homiletic "snowflake."

## 4.1. Doublets Again

A prominent church leader recently preached at an impressive ordination service on a college campus. Following the service, a group of us who were interested in preaching found ourselves around a table at the college's snack bar. As we rehearsed the sermon we had just heard, we all noticed a strange thing. At one point toward the end of the sermon, we all had difficulty recalling what had been said. It was as though our "homiletic reception antennas" had all gone on the blink at the same time. What had gone wrong? We struggled in an effort to track down what the preacher had said — this was, after all, an important closing section of the sermon. Finally, one of the group remembered a story that had been told in that section, and then another one added, "Yeah, that's right — and then we all laughed." Once we remembered the story and the laughter, however, we became even more confused, for the story itself hadn't been humorous at all.

What was going on here? After a quick check of some notes I had taken during the sermon, it became clear that the old doublet pitfall had entrapped us all. The speaker had actually told *two* stories at the climactic point in the sermon, each serving to illustrate the same meaning. Both were told well by this experienced preacher. The first story was a powerful first-person anecdote, which we eventually "got" there in the snack bar after some effort. The second story was much lighter; after its telling, a wave of chuckles and soft laughter coursed through the assembly. But since communal consciousness can seldom retain binary illustrative systems focused on a single meaning, the first-person story "stuck" with some difficulty, and everything related to the second story deleted except for the laughter. So we all attached that response to a story that oddly had no humor in it whatsoever. No wonder the preacher's climactic moment had become so garbled — we were trying to make sense of laughing at a profoundly serious story!

The lesson from this homiletic exploration in the snack bar is that more than one story illustration of any single meaning in a sermon will not work. If two are used, as in the instance just mentioned, at best only one of the two will remain in the communal consciousness. At worst, the two illustrations will fragment, with parts recombining into one new meaning, or else the doublet system will drop out of hearing entirely. *Illustration doublets simply will not work.* This principle seems to be without exception in our contemporary preaching situation.

The obvious solution is to adhere to the rule of one and only one illustration for any single meaning in a sermon. A strategy of using two illustrations anyway, with a rationale that "they'll pick out the one best suited to themselves," will encounter the same pitfall. In all likelihood, the entire location in the sermon related to that issue or single meaning will be left garbled or deleted in the congregation's consciousness. One and only one illustration for each single meaning in a sermon — that's the rule.

This rule does not need to be a vexing one for us preachers. If two or more stories have stepped forward as candidates for illustrating some meaning in our sermon, then we have the luxury of choosing between them. The runner-up stories can then be stored in our shoe box (or on our floppy disk) to be considered at some other time.

The following five guidelines will help preachers to decide which of several competing stories should be chosen:

1. The best illustration for any single meaning will address that meaning without introducing other issues and concerns.
2. The best illustration will be modest in size and will not create an "embolism" (see sec. 4.7, and also my *Narrative and Imagination,* chap. 5).
3. The best illustration will relate to the social and personal world of the widest number of hearers. It will not be arcane, appealing to only a specialized group; nor will it reflect only the preacher's world and his or her interests.
4. The best illustration will relate easily to the social and personal worlds of both women and men. A significant majority of illustrations used by male preachers are typically about males or

drawn from predominantly male experiences. Women hearing such illustrations are given the not-too-subtle message that the Gospel is not equally for them. Women are thereby forced to "translate" the illustration into their experience before it can be received by them. (I am grateful to Robert Howard for calling my attention to his research and analysis of this pervasive problem.)

5. The best illustration will be one that is fresh, speaks in a contemporary voice, and is honestly told.

*Assignment:* Even the best of today's preachers occasionally falls into the doublet pitfall in using illustrations. Look at Fred Craddock's powerful sermon "Have You Ever Heard John Preach?" in *A Chorus of Witnesses*, pp. 34–43. Reread the doublet illustrations on p. 41 (the China story and the first-person reference to the preacher's Tennessee pastorate). What single meaning is being illustrated? How do both stories relate to that single meaning?

Apply the five guidelines listed above to the doublet. Which story used alone would function best at this point in the sermon? Which story will most likely be retained by the hearers?

## For further reading

Buttrick, David. *Homiletic: Moves and Structures*, pp. 133–51. Philadelphia: Fortress Press, 1987.

Craddock, Fred B. "Have You Ever Heard John Preach?" In *A Chorus of Witnesses: Model Sermons for Today's Preacher*, ed. Thomas G. Long and Cornelius Plantinga, Jr., pp. 34–43. Grand Rapids: Wm. B. Eerdmans Publishing Co., 1994.

Eslinger, Richard. *Narrative and Imagination: Preaching the Worlds That Shape Us*. Minneapolis; Fortress Press, 1995.

Long, Thomas G. *The Witness of Preaching*, pp. 133–47. Louisville, Ky.: Westminster/John Knox Press, 1989.

## 4.2. Stories Forever

In the old topical preaching, "illustration" meant "story." The illustrations that were chosen to drive home the sermon's points were stories — the more vivid and affect-laden the better. It was (and regrettably still is) these rather extended story illustrations that "made" the sermon, that determined the sermon's evaluation, and that traveled among preachers like baseball cards being traded among kids. Everyone knew that statistics and masterful quotes were also appropriate illustrations, but it was the anecdotal reference, the story, that became almost synonymous with "illustration." In its outline, the topical sermon generally came equipped with a story illustration related to every point.

With the emergence of the new homiletics, points gradually have given way to moves, to scenes, to locations of single meaning in the homiletic plot. As noted previously, the primary distinction is that a point connoted a propositional statement appended to other propositional statements, all assuming an argumentative payoff. The single meaning of sermons within the new homiletic rarely will be propositional statements; moreover, they will form a sequence of plotted language intended to move within a congregation's hearing. "Illustrations," of necessity, are now shifting in their meaning and in their function as a consequence of this paradigm shift in preaching. No longer is the primary intent of the illustration to "ram home the proposition" and thereby make it "stick." Rather, the illustration now serves more as a catalyst for the hearers as the conceptual material forms in their consciousness. Within the preaching of the new homiletics, then, an illustration can involve a *story* that serves to illustrate the meaning or move, an *example* or *analogy,* or an *image* or *image system* (multiple images locating a single meaning).

The following guidelines offer help in working with this new and expanded role of illustrations:

First, every location of single meaning within a sermon will need to be imaged, exampled, or illustrated in order for the hearers to retain that unit of discourse. Conceptual language that is not imaged simply will not form in the congregational hearing (see sec. 4.8, "Un-Illustrations").

Second, each single meaning within a sermon can generally be illustrated by (1) a story illustration (only one per single meaning, please!), (2) an example or analogy (or a multiple set), or (3) an image or image system. The specific issues related to the single meaning or even the place of that single meaning within the homiletic plot may point the preacher toward one type of illustration and away from another. In a sermon on the prologue in John, therefore, an early move in the sermon may well deal with the darkness of the world. This early in the sermon, the preacher might decide for a series of examples of darkness rather than opting for one story focusing on an aspect of that darkness. Here, the preacher chooses to go with a scattershot approach rather than targeting one particular story illustrating darkness in the world.

Finally, as the illustrations build through the course of the sermon, be careful to vary the type used; the repetitive use of one type or one point of view will tend to diminish congregational retention. For example, to dip into the story illustration barrel repeatedly during the sermon is to wear down the hearer's capacity to remain receptive to the succession of single meanings. (This is one of the reasons attention in topical preaching dropped off so precipitously by the time the preacher was enumerating "point number four"!) Aware that the specific single meanings may be best illustrated by a variety of options from the whole palette of illustration possibilities, the preacher will want to vary the type of illustration from move to move. If we have used an image from a TV commercial (with the built-in point of view of one flopped on the couch watching the tube), we might be tempted to come up with another commercial to illustrate another move. Knowing that such repetition tends to diminish retention, however, we will look elsewhere for our illustration of the latter point.

By way of illustrating these guidelines, consider a sermon on John 9, the story of the man born blind. Let's assume that we have decided on the narrative strategy of identifying four stages in the "faith development" of this man, which we will treat as a series of moves or scenes. We may sketch the overall movement of the sermon as follows:

SCENE 1.  *"How were your eyes opened?" they asked. The man born blind has little information. "A man named Jesus," he blurts out. As to his whereabouts, he admits, "I do not know." Not much insight here. Just a name, whereabouts unknown.*

SCENE 2.  *The challenge from the religious people continues. They decide that Jesus is a sinner, since he healed on the Sabbath. Now they turn to the man born blind. "What do you say about him?" they ask. His response surprises everyone: "He is a prophet!" Whatever else, "Prophet Jesus" has been by.*

SCENE 3.  *Now the opposition grows intense. "Whose disciple are you?" they ask — "of Moses, like we are, or of this man?" As a final slur, they add, "We do not even know where he comes from." Suddenly the man born blind comes to see what they do not see. "He comes from God, that's where!" Jesus comes from God.*

SCENE 4.  *Now driven out of the synagogue, the man born blind is worse off than before. He is an outcast right there in his hometown. Now Jesus hears of his fate and seeks out the man. There is a question about the Son of Humanity, with Jesus revealing his full identity. The man now sees. He exclaims, "Lord, I believe!" Joining the new community in Christ, he worships the Word made flesh.*

Now comes the task of elaborating the content of the four scenes in the sermon, and of illustrating each one in some particular way — through an illustration, example, or image. For the first scene, I would suggest something along the lines of an excursus presenting three examples out of the lived experience of the hearers. It might look something like this:

*"Interesting how much things remain the same, isn't it? I mean, how someone can have a meeting with Jesus, maybe even have their life changed by him — baptized into his Way and his family.*

91

*Then or now, the sequence goes, "Who was it who gave such a gift?" Answer: "A man named Jesus." Question: "Where is he now?" And we hear the same refrain — "I do not know."*

*Those folks driving by this morning on the way to the beach (mountains, etc.), lots of them had something to do with Jesus at some time or other. "Where is he now?" we inquire. And the answer comes honestly, "I do not know." We might get the same answer, too, a lot closer to home. Some of us raised our children to attend worship and church school, religiously. But that was then and this is now. "Where is Jesus now?" "I don't know," some of our young adult children respond. And look, even with us, right here . . . when our faith turns routine and our church life feels flat and predictable, even for us that question about Jesus hits home. "Where is he now?" And in honesty we might have to confess, "I do not know." So that's the answer of the man born blind. Healed of his physical blindness, he still does not see Jesus, see who Jesus really is. "I do not know" is his reply.*

*Assignment:* Continue to elaborate the content of the next three scenes and to develop the imagery. Remember the options that are available. We may provide one or more images for each location (doublets excluded, of course!). Or we may provide a single example or set of examples. Finally, we may employ an illustration, a narrative anecdote (only one per move, please). But recall the variety of illustrative alternatives at our disposal. A sequence of four story illustrations is probably not the best way to locate the sermon within our contemporary experience. Images and examples are lavishly available to the preacher. If we do pick a story illustration, we will discover that it will function more powerfully when it is part of a diverse illustrative system.

*For further reading*

Brown, Raymond. *The Gospel according to John.* 2 vols. Garden City, N.Y.: Doubleday, 1966.
O'Day, Gail R. *Revelation in the Fourth Gospel: Narrative Mode and Theological Claim.* Philadelphia: Fortress Press, 1986.

## 4.3. Creeping Illustrations

A gifted seminarian preached her concluding sermon for the Intro to Preaching course. Everything went quite well except for one problem — the class could not recall the entire opening section of the sermon following her introduction. Everyone seemed to hang on the edge of the last sentence of her opening, but they didn't know where they had gone next. When asked to consult her sermon manuscript, the preacher pointed to the following paragraphs, where the problem occurred. Can you detect what went wrong?

> *There are times in life when things get tough. We're going along, maybe without a care in the world, and all of a sudden, it hits — disaster. Or maybe it comes on slowly, this impending trouble. We may not even spot its early warning signs. But sooner or later things are really different, badly different. The people in the Bible had a name for it — this disruption, this turmoil — "exile." Exile is when you feel no longer at home and it feels like you can never return there again. Exile is thinking everything is all right and then disaster hits, robbing you of that security. Doing time in exile is hard time, for Israel and for us.*
>
> *A friend of mine found herself in exile. All of a sudden, she learned that she was being laid off from her secretarial job, a job she really loved. Now she was "away from home" even while sitting around the house waiting for news of a nibble from one of the applications she had made for a new job. Even her home felt different. She could not return to the job she loved, to her co-workers who were so much fun, . . . all of it, gone. It's easy to feel depressed,*

*like God has abandoned you, when you land in exile. Finally, after much prayer and thought, she decided to move, to go back to school and study journalism. And guess what? Three years later she's working on the staff of a big newspaper in Nashville. Recently she wrote and said, "I thank God now for being laid off from my old job. What a wonderful future God had in store for me. I thank God every day!"*

*So we may be going along, with everything seeming OK. Then that time called exile hits. And all of a sudden we're in a place called "not home."*

The pitfall here is that of the creeping illustration. The illustration has "crept" away from the single meaning at stake in the move. Up to the point of the clause "when you land in exile" in the middle paragraph, the illustration of the woman's job loss nicely illustrates the single meaning centering on the experience of exile. The elements of not feeling at home, of not being able to return to a status quo ante, of feeling loss — all these are aptly illustrated in this portrayal of a friend's loss of a job she loved.

Notice, however, that the story does not end with the friend in exile. Our preacher continued the story through to its positive ending, in another city, after the friend's initiative to attend school. None of the material after "Finally, after much prayer and thought . . ." illustrates the conceptual meaning related to exile. In fact, the possibility of exercising personal initiative to rectify the situation and the move to a new location with its new vocation all suggest the opposite of the notion of being in exile. The illustration has crept away from its original location — that of illustrating exile — and crawled to a new place illustrating a very blessed situation of restoration.

With the hearers now led to that new place by the illustration, it was impossible to bring them back to the move's intended meaning, which dealt with the experience of exile. Now, finding themselves hearing dissonant meanings between the conceptual material (related to exile) and the ending of the illustration (restoration), they could form no single meaning. The first, and rather important, segment of the sermon thus dropped entirely out of their hearing.

> *Assignment:* Recover a sequence of your recent sermons, either on manuscript or on audio tape. Identify all of the narrative illustrations you used along with the single meanings they were intended to illustrate. Now scrutinize the accumulated list for any evidence of creeping illustrations. If you discover this pitfall lurking in your list, pause to note the corrections necessary so you can avoid this problem in the future.

## 4.4. The "I" of the Illustration

How — or even whether — to use first-person stories in preaching is one of the most controversial questions in contemporary homiletics. Is self-reference by the preacher a mark of emotional honesty, solidarity with the life experiences of the congregation, and a repudiation of pulpit authoritarianism? Or are "I" stories signs of emotional overindulgence and manipulation, their use a disregard of the effects of such references upon the hearers? A cursory reading of opinions on this question reveals a striking difference of opinion. Tom Long nicely states the divergence today in views on first-person pulpit reference:

> Contemporary homileticians and other students of preaching have given several answers to that question, ranging from an enthusiastic yes ("The best help we can offer is our own woundedness and a description of what has saved and healed us" — Salmon), through a cautious "sometimes" ("self-disclosure in moderation is appropriate to preaching" — Craddock), to a horrified no ("To be blunt, there are virtually no good reasons to talk about ourselves from the pulpit" — Buttrick). (*The Witness of Preaching*, p. 177)

It is not enough simply to conclude from this range of opinion that the best policy is to proceed with the use of such stories in moderation. The question is not one of achieving a golden mean in first-person stories, for some types of personal reference will *always* result in defeated intentions. Here we must disagree with Tom Long's assessment that "far more important than a list of rules is the matter of intent" (*The Witness of Preaching,* pp. 177–78). Let's grant a generous presumption regarding the intent of nearly every preacher's first-person references. Some will nevertheless evoke responses either disconnected from that intent or even at cross-purposes with it. Pitfalls abound in the "I-illustrations," and merely having fine intentions is no protection against these homiletic disasters. We must probe deeper, both by way of analyzing the dynamics of first-person pulpit references and through articulating some rather specific norms for use of the preacherly "I," if we are going to use it at all. First, though, let's look at the kinds of "I-illustrations" that almost always will defeat our best intentions.

## Preacher-as-Hero/Victim Stories

Among aviation buffs, a pilot's heroic self-reference story is characteristically prefaced by the phrase "There I was. . . ." In fact, a considerable amount of humor in those circles begins with these three words. For preachers to present themselves as heroic is both as easily detected (even without the stereotyped phrase) and as equally parodied.

Beyond this problem, though, a profound theological issue obtains whenever the preacher presents himself or herself as the hero — namely, the presentation will always be in ironic relationship to the Gospel. Preacher-as-hero stories are the modern expression of the pharisaical self-display castigated by Jesus repeatedly. To those who wear their fringes long — and who present themselves as pulpit heroes — Jesus has this condemnation, "They do not practice what they teach" (Matt. 23:3).

With the triumph of the therapeutic in the churches these days, it is much more likely that we will hear first-person references in which the preacher exposes some personal wounds, abuses, or other psychic pains. A dynamic will be encountered here that will inevitably skew homiletic intention. We may speak of this pitfall as "the defeat of congregational expectation." It goes as follows.

96

Almost every parish extends to its preacher an implicitly valorized homiletic role. In other words, a congregation likes to think highly of its preacher. To a certain extent, this tendency is self-serving, for a congregation gains in its own self-esteem in relation to its pastor-preacher. This valorization, which is mostly implicit, has little to do with whether a congregant "liked the pastor's sermon this morning." Rather, it persists — except in seriously dysfunctional pastor-parish situations — whether the preacher is received warmly, tepidly, or coolly, homiletically speaking.

For the preacher to adopt the stance of victim in the pulpit is both to repudiate the conventional role expectation held by the congregation and to evoke a reaction to the homiletic deprivation. The preacher-as-victim story is therefore really an "anti-story," running in opposition to the implicit valorization held by the hearers. Hearing a story that undermines this role expectation destabilizes the relationship of pastor and parish, and it also calls into question the dominant congregational self-image. The result will often be a sense of anger and resentment, either of a free-floating sort (which will probably fix itself Velcro-like to some quite unrelated issue in pastor-parish relations) or as an immediate negative response to the victim story. In this area we must agree with Buttrick's assessment: there are no good reasons for pulpit promulgations of the preacher-as-victim. (I am indebted to Marilyn and Robert Howard for their helpful analysis of this point.)

## Personal References

Most of us who are called to preach have some sort of personal interests in which we engage and in which we find fulfillment and meaning. Naturally, our imagination will return again and again to these personal interests when seeking images and examples within a sermon. In sharing our personal hobby, sport, or whatever, the first problem is that we will tend to bring it up in the majority of our sermons. Having become chronic, further references from the pulpit to our personal interest will tend to add nothing positive to our sermons. At best, the latest variant on the theme will create a fond little intermission from the ongoing movement of the sermon; less positively, such a reference tends to precipitate instant boredom.

Other issues are at stake, however, in the chronic recital of personal interests during our sermons. In some cases, a whole value system comes along with our anecdotes. Football and other highly competitive and violent American sports import all sorts of alien values within the context of Christian worship and preaching. In other instances, our personal interest may be so gender- or class-specific as to render it inappropriate for preaching. (A pastor's "monster truck" fetish really will not go over very well in a university church setting; likewise an addiction to scuba diving will not play well in a rural church in the Midwest.) Finally, we may well examine why such personal references have become a regular diet within our sermons at all. Are we perhaps really using these anecdotes to say, "Please like me, church people!" every Lord's Day? If so, our problem is more extensive than that of homiletics.

### Overpowering First-Person Stories

When particularly powerful first-person references are told from the pulpit, a predictable series of responses can be identified. Like the detonation of a neutron bomb, these strong, affect-ladened stories have several unmistakable consequences. On one hand, they are most likely to be retained in congregational memory — often for years. ("Rev. Smith? Isn't she the one who watched her mother die when she was a kid? When did she serve here . . . the early eighties, wasn't it?") On the other hand, these overpowered personal stories will totally blow away their surrounding sermonic context. ("What was Rev. Smith's sermon really about that day?" Then or now, who knows?)

Perhaps we are tempted to use such a first-person story by the thought that at least *this* illustration will be retained by our hearers. We are certainly correct in our hunch that the powerful first-person story will be remembered. We are mistaken, however, if we believe such overpowering stories will illustrate anything other than ourselves.

## Traits of Positive First-Person References

Besides these consistently disastrous uses of the pulpit first person, there are other, happier examples. If we examine the first-person illustrations and examples that do work as intended, we find several characteristics held in common across the span of theological and liturgical diversity in the churches.

One trait of a homiletically successful first-person experience is that *it is representative of the lived experience of the hearers.* When the African American preacher speaks of his or her experience growing up in America, the power of that story is in its representative character for the members of the congregation. The story will be recognized immediately as "our story," both for those who have had quite similar experiences and for those who may have not but who share in a communal identity with those who have. This trait of representative identity can be extended beyond the particular context of the African American church; even though our representative identity is now quite diminished in the majority churches, there remain incidents and experiences the preacher does hold in common with the congregation. We are on relatively thin ice today in this regard, however. The representative role of the preacher continues to erode in many of the churches, and no general rule can decide how any particular first-person anecdote will function. If the illustration does not rather quickly receive a responsive nod from the congregation, signifying, "Yes, this is our story," then the preacher will wind up illustrating only the preacher, to the detriment of the sermon.

A second trait of the successful first-person story is that *the point of view is one experienced by the hearers as well as the preacher.* If the story begins, "Last week, I was walking down the mall and saw a bunch of kids outside the video-game place . . . ," in all probability the hearers can move in to share the preacher's experience. Notice at this point, however, just how disposable the first-person point of view is to such a shared experience. Since the effectiveness of the anecdote hangs on the hearers' experiencing it with some real immediacy, the first-person reference only serves to delay that common reference point. Why not begin that story, "Did you ever walk down the mall and see a bunch of kids outside the video-game

99

hangout . . . ?" In either performance, though, the story will be effective to the extent that the experience and the point of view can be held in common with the congregation.

A third and critically important trait of an effective first-person illustration is that *it must have the ring of honesty about it.* So many examples exist of questionable first-person pulpit stories that this issue of homiletic integrity must be raised. Most of us have heard stories of preachers who "borrow" an anecdote from others and portray it as their own. And a fair percentage of the faithful who attend to Christian preaching have heard the same story from different pastoral leaders who delivered it from the pulpit as their own experience. This pulpit plagiarism robs the offending preacher of integrity and also extends its damage to us all. Given the host of issues in which clergy are under attack these days (in many instances quite deservedly), we certainly must abstain from this homiletic promiscuity "henceforth and forever more"! Paul Scott Wilson gives us preachers a blunt, relevant warning: "The preacher must never lie; or claim that something is factual that is fictional; or say that something was a personal experience that was not; or disclose something that was told in confidence" (*The Practice of Preaching,* p. 265).

Examples of a lack of pulpit honesty, then, include a familiar list of transgressions: claiming someone else's experience as your own; revealing confidential matters from your present or past arenas of ministry; demeaning or stereotyping others in any illustrations, including those in the first person. It is no accident that many of the issues related to honesty in preaching have to do with abuses of first-person references. Perhaps this should tell us something about their power, as well as caution us to use them only with homiletic care and moral integrity.

*Assignment:* Identify the last first-person story you used in your preaching. Evaluate it according to this discussion of types of "I" illustrations. Did your illustration function to enable, deflect, or defeat your intention in choosing it in the first place? If necessary, how would you alter your "I" illustration to increase the possibility of its functioning effectively? Would a shift in point of view help, or perhaps a move from first person to second (from "I" to "you")?

## For further reading

Buttrick, David. *Homiletic: Moves and Structures,* pp. 141–43. Philadelphia: Fortress Press, 1987.

Eslinger, Richard. *Narrative and Imagination: Preaching the Worlds That Shape Us,* chap. 5. Minneapolis: Fortress Press, 1995.

Long, Thomas G. *The Witness of Preaching.* Louisville, Ky.: Westminster/John Knox Press, 1989.

Thulin, Richard. *The "I" of the Sermon.* Minneapolis: Fortress Press, 1989. Presents an alternative view on first-person pulpit reference.

Wilson, Paul Scott. *The Practice of Preaching,* pp. 263–67. Nashville: Abingdon Press, 1995.

## 4.5. At Cross-Purposes

Imagine that you are preparing to preach on the Johannine passage in which Jesus announces, "I am the vine, you are the branches" (John 15:5). Now suppose that you decide to plot the sermon so that three moves, or sections, explore how both in American culture and in the American church, the dominant attitude is "Branches don't need vines." The individualism of our culture shapes the ways in which we do politics, articulate self-improvement and pop psychology, and construe Christian life. A sequence of moves in this series would describe this "vineless branches" syndrome in society and then within the church and would conclude with an analysis of the resultant loneliness and despair that presently abounds. This analysis would focus on the placebo many people turn to — that of living their lives through a vicarious identification with cultural and countercultural heroes.

Given this three-move series, it becomes rather easy to image or illustrate these aspects of the vineless branches syndrome. We have, then, a sequence that proceeds as follows:

MOVE 1. *"Who needs vines?" the world shouts. "Be a branch; be all that you can be! Choose a lifestyle, elevate your consciousness, look out for number one!" (Image: Bumper sticker on expensive car at marina that reads, "The one who dies with the most toys wins.")*

MOVE 2. *In the church, too, we can hear this same message — "Get yourself saved, fixed and right with God." Success can be yours; all you need to do is try God. "He's the real thing!" (Image: Cartoon showing new church building with huge marquee announcing, "Church-O-Plex," which lists types of worship available from "traditional" to "contemporary," "New Age," "Holy Communion," etc., etc.)*

MOVE 3. *So look around now at all these vineless branches . . . look at all the lonely people. Lonely and lost, living their lives through someone else. (Illustration: Suicide of Nirvana rock star Kurt Cobain; despair of his fans, including one whose own suicide note lamented, "When Kurt Cobain died, I died with him.")*

Consider now moves 4 and 5, which will conclude this sermon. We shift first to the Johannine affirmation in which Jesus says to us, "I am the true vine." Then we shape a move based on the Lord's command that we must "bear much fruit." Included within this last move will be the emphasis on joy found in 15:11. The central question here is how to image or illustrate this two-move series.

Almost without thinking, we may be tempted to illustrate the "true vine" move by pointing to some "false vines" such as drug abuse or messianic claimants like David Koresh. The fifth move, on bearing much fruit, may similarly find us thinking of illustrations of churches where fruitfulness is not present. (We could mention declining church membership, factionalism, and church-dividing schisms.) Proceeding in this manner, however, within a sermon whose homiletic plot is both clear and effective, would involve us in a pitfall related to illustrations. The positive moves would be illustrated or imaged through negative examples; the moves and the examples would be at cross-purposes with each other.

One of the most prevalent tendencies in sermon illustration is to image aspects of darkness, evil, injustice, and sin very dramatically and effectively but then to come up dry when turning to light, grace, healing, fruitfulness, and reconciliation. Let's face it — as preachers today, it is a lot easier to illustrate the various dimensions of the unredeemed world than it is to speak concretely of the realities of the Gospel. This disparity may be the primary reason that we wind up illustrating at cross-purposes, employing negative examples related to positive concepts. The opposite problem of matching positive illustrations with negative moves is not nearly as common, perhaps because the negative examples come much more easily to mind.

We may speak of this pitfall as a "Gospel-deficit" problem in illustration. It is not that we do not talk about the Gospel; the problem is more that of generating image and illustration systems that effectively concretize the Good News. Lacking such positive illustrations, we may stoop to using negative examples for positive, gospel moves in the sermon. That will not work. The resultant preaching becomes confused and garbled for the hearers. Lamentably, the portions of the sermon related to law, sin, and darkness nicely form within the congregation's mind. The portions related to God's reign and life in Christ remain vague and remote. To avoid this problem we must follow an inflexible rule: *Image positive meanings with positive illustrations, and negative meanings with negative examples.*

Consider now some possible approaches to illustration with regard to the final two moves related to John 15:1-11. First, we develop the conceptual content:

MOVE 4. *Jesus speaks different words to us . . . "I am the vine,"
he says, "and you are the branches." That wonderful
word "abide" now is heard. We branches are asked to
"abide" in the true vine, to "remain," to "locate ourselves," to "find a home in." It is the vine that gives us
life, all of us branches. This true vine connects all of us
to each other, branches of the same true vine. A branch
without a vine withers and dies; it is no longer connected
to what gives life.*

MOVE 5. *Now comes the command . . . direct from the Vine to us
branches. "Bear much fruit," says the Lord. "That is the
sign of your abiding in me." It is our calling to be fruitful.*

Next we must illustrate the conceptual material in some way.
Our conceptual and analytic language has been extended as far as
possible without the hearers drifting off and losing attention. Recall
that our options are to (1) provide an illustration (only one per
move!), (2) offer one or more examples, or (3) image the scene out
of the lived experience of the hearers. Whichever we decide upon,
we will match positive with positive, and strength with strength.
(This move or sermon section is crucial to the sermon. It therefore
must be imaged strongly.)

Since the fourth move deals with the true vine, itself a strong
image, it may be difficult to provide concretion through the use
of other imagery. For example, to image (in a concrete but lu-
dicrous fashion) each Christian as a computer station all connected
to the Mainframe called Jesus might lead to a clash in image
systems!

Assume, to leap ahead, that we have chosen a set of examples
from local congregational life to image the final move of the
sermon, dealing with fruit-bearing. These have briefly identified
ways in which we are as a people in fact bearing fruit with joy. In
one parish setting I was recently part of, I might have pointed to
our church's Teen Feed program to homeless youth, the joy-filled
life and work of the campus ministry community in our midst,
and the outreach to the unchurched, which included an invitation
to a new, contemporary worship service called Early Christians.

This three-example set is quite manageable within the final move of the sermon.

If we do decide to use this threefold example in the fifth move, then we would want to steer clear of using a similar example system for move 4. To repeat the kind of illustration used weakens the entire series and progressively diminishes the impact of each succeeding illustration system.

In the fourth move, then, we seem to be left with the options of either expanding on the vine image itself or selecting an appropriate illustration. How would you proceed at this point? (*Hint:* Local churches within traditions where frequent, joyful Communion is the practice may provide the preacher "natural" imagery related to the text's image of the true vine. And communities of faith where members gather in small groups for devotional Bible study also offer ready imagery regarding the branches and the vine.)

*For further reading*

Buttrick, David. *Homiletic: Moves and Structures,* pp. 135–38. Philadelphia: Fortress Press, 1987.

## 4.6. Term Papers and Slide Shows

A number of issues surround sermon illustration that are not related directly to the illustration's content, point of view, or sense of immediacy. These issues deal with the presentation of the illustration, example, or image, which in itself can severely diminish effectiveness. How we introduce an illustration may even, in fact, become part of its meaning. In the case of narrative illustration, our introductory remarks almost always work to enhance or detract from the story. The main problematics here are pitfalls I have labeled "term papers and slide shows."

## Term Paper-itis

Many of us with seminary education come away from that experience financially poorer but also marvelously equipped to do scholarship. We have written so many papers that we may feel we could produce the next edition of the *Chicago Manual of Style* all by ourselves. Most of all, we have been formed within a community whose norms include appropriate attribution and where one of the deadliest sins is plagiarism. So we footnote everything we have cited and take care not to let someone else's ideas be presented as our own. All of this is meet, right, and salutary within the context of theological education. A sermon, however, is not a seminary term paper.

You have perhaps heard sermons where every reference or illustration was excessively attributed. Before a quotation is given, the preacher prefaces it with some footnote-like remarks. *"Rebecca Chopp, professor of theology and now dean at Candler Divinity School in Atlanta, has written in her book on feminist theology,* The Praxis of Suffering, *this statement. . . ."* Or we might hear a preacher introduce some statistics with, *"Every four years, our national church office on education sends out questionnaires on camping programs in every presbytery. The report that compiles those findings is called* Camping Alive! *and is distributed throughout the denomination and used in planning future directions in camping. In the present issue of* Camping Alive! *an alarming statistic is found on page 37. . . ."*

In the former case, Dean Chopp's distinguished resume is mostly deleted by the hearers as it is spoken — the material is simply not heard. By the time the preacher has concluded this introductory citation, even the quotation itself is in jeopardy. So while we need to make some remark to indicate attribution (after all, *we* did not write *The Praxis of Suffering!*), the best results are obtained from minimal comments. *"A seminary dean recently wrote that . . ."* or *"A theologian recently put it this way. . . ."* If the dean's gender is important to communicate, one strategy is to fold these pieces of information in as we go along. *"So, when Dean Chopp speaks about suffering, she is raising a really important question, isn't she?"* It is probably not important to present in our preface to the quotation information regarding Atlanta and the name of the seminary. Given these cautions regarding the citing of the Chopp quotation, a revision of the *Camping Alive!* reference comes readily to mind: *"In a new report on camping, it says that. . . ."*

## Slide Show-itis

There is a tendency for preachers to get chatty while prefacing an illustration. This tendency is compounded when our egos get in the way and may result in something like the following. *"Jim White is one of the top United Methodist scholars in the field of worship. He teaches at Notre Dame in Indiana, but he really is a Vermonter. When I was over at his house last fall, he showed me his wonderful collection of New England crafts. Well, Jim wrote in the* Circuit Rider *recently that when United Methodists worship, they. . . ."* This sounds for all the world like the comments made by the Joneses at their endless slide show on their trip to Europe last summer. *"Now here is another shot of the town center of Pretzelburg. Alice is standing by the fountain, see her? She's holding up one of those giant pretzels they make there. It must be a foot in diameter. The shop where we got them is off to the left there. See the sign 'Das Pretzelhaus' up in the corner?"* (And on and on . . .)

If these kinds of rambling, semipersonal comments preface illustrative material, notice two outcomes. First, the congregation may experience frustration and even anger. Second, the effect will be most likely to render the whole illustrative section fuzzy. The reason has to do with a split in focus. In our ramblings before the quotation from James White, we have begun assembling a congregational point of view looking at the Vermonter's living room and the crafts he has on display. After establishing that point of view, we suddenly present a statement on worship and expect the hearers to detach themselves from a focus on the living room and attend to an insight he has written on liturgics. The split in point of view is compounded, since we have established a *visual* perspective regarding the living room and then shift to an *aural* perspective, expecting people to hear a quotation. The rapid shift in both point of view and sensory mode is boggling; no one will get the quotation. The rule here is the same as for term paper-itis: a minimal ascription is generally the best. So Professor White's living room, along with our recent visit to his home, must be deleted for the sake of his comment on worship.

### For further reading

Chopp, Rebecca S. *The Praxis of Suffering: An Interpretation of Liberation and Political Theologies*. Maryknoll, N.Y.: Orbis Books, 1986.
White, James F. *Introduction to Christian Worship*. Rev. ed. Nashville: Abingdon Press, 1990.

## 4.7. The Dreaded Embolism

*Big illustrations will usually detach from content and thus defeat themselves.*

David Buttrick, *Homiletic*

One of the most prevalent pitfalls in preaching is the tendency for an illustration to expand to the extent that (1) its illustrative purpose is thwarted and (2) the congregation becomes entrapped in the illustration's vast anecdotal world. One of the primary criteria of narrative illustrations is that the congregation may easily enter that narrative context and, after it's been given, just as easily reenter the sermonic plot and move on. An illustration can all too easily become like an embolism, however, going off on its own and expanding into a story-world in which the hearers become enmeshed. The embolism thus no longer serves to illustrate any single meaning whatsoever. Rather, a succession of meanings or implications is projected in congregational consciousness as the story is developed. The hearers may attend to the variety of analogies within the story, but each of those analogies also may be discarded one by one as the narrative progresses. (Embolism illustrations are typically too complex to refer to any single meaning; in fact, we really should not refer to them as illustrations at all.) In many instances, the underlying purpose of the embolism may be simply to convey an affect to the hearers. Such a story's "point" is the set of feelings evoked by the elaborate anecdote.

Let's look at an example of these sermon embolisms in order to become more skilled in spotting and avoiding their dreaded outcomes. In a sermon on the unity of the church, one preacher looked for an illustration to illumine the necessity of reconciliation in Christ. A story was found about a Baptist church in Jerusalem that was burned down by Jewish extremists but rebuilt with the help of compassionate Jews in the Holy City. Within the sermon as preached, this story occupied about one-third of the total sermonic material — too extensive for the congregation to recall what the main point of telling the story was (too many possible meanings) or what the sermon dealt with apart from the story.

Watch as the possible meanings come to mind in the story's telling but then must be laid aside as the story continues to develop.

| The story | Congregational responses |
| --- | --- |
| 1. The first section of the story as preached dealt with the way Jerusalem is divided into Muslim, Jewish, and Christian quarters. A group of Jewish extremists are introduced who take offense at a small Baptist church operating in the Jewish sector of the city. One night they break into the church, spread gasoline around, and burn the church to the ground. | The initial thoughts of the congregation as the people follow the story deal with the identity of these Jewish extremists and their motivation for attacking the little congregation's church. Some resistance may emerge within hearers who have concerns that the story is leading to an anti-Semitic conclusion. |
| 2. The story continues with the heroic struggle of that small Baptist congregation. Under the leadership of their young pastor, they gather in the midst of the ruins to support each other and to pray. | The hearers can now vividly "see" the scene in their minds. We can smell the faint smoke and hear the crunch of the charred wood underfoot. Affective responses may range from anger (at "the Jews") to compassion for the little congregation. |

109

3. Now the story continues with the word about the church's fate making the daily newspaper. The Jewish community rises up in concern. A rabbi offers his synagogue for the church's worship. The mayor of the city of Jerusalem offers help, and a building fund is set up in a Jewish bank. Leaders of the city join in the ground-breaking ceremony for the fine new church facility.

Our focus is now on the positive steps to reconciliation and rebuilding between the leadership of the Jewish community and the Baptist congregation. Congregational response is now more relaxed and reassured. A happy ending has occurred, in spite of the violent action of the extremists.

After telling the story, the preacher went on to extol the virtue of reconciliation, which has come to its fulfillment in Jesus Christ. In retrospect, however, little of this homiletic material was communicated to the hearers. The extended story most certainly did "stick," but it was retained with an assemblage of meanings quite incidental to those intended by the preacher.

The conclusion is inevitable regarding such embolisms in the sermon. With Richard Lischer, we must concur that "illustrations often assume a life of their own, and neither the preacher nor the congregation can remember what they were illustrations *of*" ("Preaching as the Church's Language," p. 124). These oversized stories will predictably rule the sermon, quite apart from whatever uses the preacher had for them as illustrations.

*For further reading*

Eslinger, Richard. *Narrative and Imagination: Preaching the Worlds That Shape Us,* chap. 5. Minneapolis: Fortress Press, 1995.

Lischer, Richard. "Preaching as the Church's Language." In *Listening to the Word: Studies in Honor of Fred B. Craddock,* ed. Gail R. O'Day and Thomas G. Long, pp. 113–30. Nashville: Abingdon Press, 1993.

## 4.8. Un-Illustrations

*The images bear the meaning of the sermon rather than illustrate it.*

Thomas Troeger, *Imagining a Sermon*

If a popular beverage could be recently marketed as the Un-cola, then in the realm of preaching we could well speak of the pitfall of "un-illustrations." The problem is essentially a lack of awareness of how particular and concrete we preachers need to make illustrations, examples, and images before they are able to form within the congregation's consciousness. Studies in the dynamics of congregational retention show that after a relatively brief period, unimaged sermonic discourse is lost almost as soon as it is spoken. The hearers really do not hear discursive language after a shockingly short amount of time; unimaged, the language does not form and is not retained. One aspect of this pitfall of failing to bring pulpit speech to concretion and immediacy is that the preacher is often unaware that he or she is in trouble at this point. As we considered in section 1.1, the problem is that the language remains "talking about" rather than a "speaking of."

Imagine that you have come to a clergy workshop on preaching. The focus of the morning's session is on this issue of imaging and illustration. As a test case, the leader invites the group to consider the steps or moves in the parable of the barren fig tree (Luke 13:6-9). The group has structured this little parable into a number of scenes that will become the sequence of the sermon, and now it is brainstorming as to the imaging of the first scene, which is the problem of barrenness in the vineyard. Our insightful preacher-homileticians have already spotted the ecclesial context of this first step or scene and therefore know that illustrations and images will need to be drawn from life within the church. After a time of working in small groups, the workshop leader calls everyone back together, and they share their thoughts about the possible imaging of this scene:

GROUP 1. *"We came up with two images. First, we agreed on the shortage of finances in the church, both at a local level and at the judicatory level. Then we also felt that one feature of barrenness in the vineyard has to do with the slow membership decline most all of us are experiencing. That is an important one."* (murmurs of assent from the others)

GROUP 2. *"Our group talked a lot about the division of the church into factions, mainly the split between liberals and evangelicals. We hardly talk to each other any more . . . it's all power politics, each side acting to hold onto its power and to take away power from the other."* (more murmurs of assent)

GROUP 3. *"We looked at how so many churches are focused on their own survival, their own problems, that they hardly take any time any more to reach out to the world. If there is barrenness in the vineyard, it's really about our preoccupation with ourselves."* (comments of assent like "That's right" and "Preach it, sister!")

The workshop leader has been busy scribbling these findings onto the inevitable newsprint. When the recording is completed, the leader makes the following evaluation: "Now these thoughts are all right on target; all of the groups have hit on really important dimensions of our barrenness as God's people. Only one problem here, though. We have not yet crossed the threshold from 'talk about' to an 'imaging of' any of the issues. If we get only this close,

112

our listeners will not get what we are saying; it will evaporate instead of being retained."

There are looks of confusion and frustration in the gathering. One preacher asks, "I don't get it. What have we done wrong?" The leader responds, "None of what we have accumulated here is 'wrong,' folks. It's just that we have not yet imaged any of our analysis so that our listeners can experience it for themselves. Let's take the first group's insights. Look at this business of membership decline. Once we state this issue and elaborate it briefly, we'll really need to make it seen or heard or felt, . . . remembered or experienced in some way. In your church, how do those who will hear this sermon bump into this problem of decline? What are some of the images in congregational life that bring this issue to concrete immediacy?"

Rev. Jones answers, "The empty pews we have every Sunday morning, maybe except for Christmas and Easter."

Rev. Garcia adds, "Yeah, and the memory of when they were filled and who used to fill them!"

Rev. Koenig adds, "It's also the *age* of who's still there. The pews are empty where the young adults and their children should be. Even the children of those who still faithfully attend have dropped out."

Rev. Brown then jumps in: "It's not just the empty pews, it's trying to recruit enough people for all the jobs we have to do. Nominations time is a nightmare."

Rev. Lee comments: "We don't have this problem in our Korean congregation. All the pews are filled when we start church on Sunday afternoon, with people of all ages, including those young adults and their children. But we do know that our host congregation is having this problem, . . . very seriously having this problem."

The workshop leader hops back in. "OK. I think we have enough to work with here. What we'll need to do is to provide a point of view on this for our hearers and then let them reexperience what they already have known for some time. So our decisions now regard what we invite the hearers to see and hear, touch and feel. How would this work as our opening scene in the sermon plot? Let's try one approach to scene 1."

*There is barrenness in the vineyard. A lack of fruitfulness in much of the church. It's marked by a lot of looking back to some "good old days." . . . Looking back instead of looking ahead. Take the decline in members in our church, our [conference, presbytery, diocese], our denomination. It just keeps happening, year after year. In spite of all the talk and the programs, nothing seems to turn it around. You know, not everything we do in church is written out in our order of worship. We begin with "The Prelude." But more honestly, we should add, "The entering of the sanctuary and the looking around at the empty pews." Then it should read, "The remembering of those dear saints who are absent from us in death." Then our bulletins could read, "The awareness that most of us are on the older side and that there aren't many young adults here, including our own grown children." Then, we would list, "The realization that some other churches are busting at the seams." Finally, these preparations for worship could conclude with, "The feeling of anger, guilt, and frustration." What a way to begin worship of the living God! But that is how it is when the vineyard lacks fruitfulness . . . when things get flat. There is barrenness in the vineyard.*

The workshop leader asks the group what the point of view is for the imaging. Immediately the answer comes, "Entering church, sitting down before worship, and looking at the bulletin."

Another participant chimes in, "But as the worshiper is invited to look at the 'real' headings related to membership decline, there is some implied perspective on the deceased parishioners and on absent children."

Someone else asks the workshop leader, "Was it intentional that you used a church bulletin point of view when studies show that many growing churches have abandoned printed bulletins entirely?"

The leader winks and announces, "I see it's now time for lunch. When we return, we'll look at the second scene in our parable, the one related to the 'cutting down' business. How are we going to image that? See you at 1:30."

114

*For further reading*

Benedict, Daniel C., and Craig K. Miller. *Contemporary Worship for the Twenty-First Century: Worship or Evangelism?* Nashville: Discipleship Resources, 1994.

Buttrick, David. *Homiletic: Moves and Structures,* pp. 127–70. Philadelphia: Fortress Press, 1987.

Fitzgerald, George R. *A Practical Guide to Preaching,* esp. chap. 6, "Images in Preaching: A Theatre in Your Head." New York: Paulist Press, 1980.

Scott, Bernard Brandon. *Hear Then the Parable: A Commentary on the Parables of Jesus.* Minneapolis: Fortress Press, 1989.

Taylor, Barbara Brown. "Preaching the Body." In *Listening to the Word: Studies in Honor of Fred B. Craddock,* ed. Gail R. O'Day and Thomas G. Long, pp. 207–21. Nashville: Abingdon Press, 1993.

Troeger, Thomas H. *Imagining a Sermon.* Nashville: Abingdon Press, 1990.

## 4.9. Lack of Perspective

*Lack of point-of-view control is a major cause of congregations that hear, but do not hear, sermons.*

David Buttrick, *Homiletic*

Imagine a process of sermon preparation in which the preacher is searching for a way to image or illustrate Paul's notion "the wisdom of this world" in 1 Corinthians 1:18-25. Our preacher (known as Pastor John to the children of his parish) decides that he will focus on the culture's fixation on knowledge to the exclusion of any truth claims — a stance of objectivity and control. After considering several other examples, he recalls a retreat setting at which one of the lecturers — a seminary dean — mentioned that a regional accrediting agency had revised its extensive policy statement by deleting all references to "the search for truth" and substituting "the pursuit of knowledge." A Christian seminary, he remembered the

115

dean remarking, will find it impossible to go with the spirit of the times and abandon its commitment to the truth of the Gospel.

With such thoughts in his mind, Pastor John typed the illustration of Paul's "wisdom of the world" into his Macintosh as follows:

> It's pretty clear these days that folks are interested in "knowledge" rather than "truth." Today, the wisdom of the world is into technology, with its ability to organize and control. Just what all this worldly wisdom is for, what its purpose is, remains unclear. Our regional accrediting agency for all of higher education including our seminaries, for example, just came out with revised guidelines. At every point where the document used to read "search for truth" it now reads "pursuit of knowledge." Here is the wisdom of the world today, still looking for control, still grasping for worldly power.

The pitfall here is a bit subtle. There is no problem with the example taken from the preacher's experience at the retreat. The accrediting agency's shift in phraseology is an all too disturbing example of the spirit of the age. Rather, the homiletic problem relates to an absence of point of view with regard to the example. Much of the illustrative material used in our preaching is simply fed back to the hearers without providing any real point of view or perspective. Since it is difficult for congregations to add a point of view to illustrations or imagery, the effect is that a certain immediacy is never achieved. The illustrations, examples, and images remain vague and lack concretion.

Fortunately, Pastor John spotted the problem with the example's weak point of view. He still liked the reference to the shift from truth to knowledge in the story, so he began to explore possible points of view. First, and most obvious, was his own hearing of the story at the retreat. Thus he could begin, "As most of you know, I was on retreat last week at Mercy Center. During one of the sessions the speaker told us a disturbing story that had just been learned at the seminary." This approach was immediately rejected because the first-person point of view would have his listeners focused on him and his retreat experience. It would then be difficult to move that point of view to the accrediting agency's policy shift.

Then the pastor tried putting the congregation itself in the position of a seminary dean who opened the mailing from the agency and read the report with its shifts. "Now we're getting warm," he thought. Still, this point of view (the dean's experience of opening the report and reading it) exposed other agendas, including a turbulent past history of that congregation during a pastorate by one of the seminary's graduates.

So once more Pastor John dumped the revised point of view from his computer. Just then he had an inspiration based on what he had just done on the Macintosh. The finished example story with its built-in point of view went like this:

> *A staff member of the regional accrediting agency just got back to his office from their annual meeting in Atlanta. There had been a delightful shift in the agency's policy that would affect every college, university, and even seminary in the South. He couldn't wait to see what the revised policy would look like, so he pulled up the old policy on his computer. Every place the document had the phrase "search for truth," he highlighted and hit the delete command. Hitting another command made the phrase "pursuit of knowledge" pop into view on the screen. "There," he thought to himself, "now that looks much better!"*

Now the story had a built-in point of view — a staff person working at his computer. The congregation could easily "look on" as the changes were made in the policy document, could "see" the old phrase being deleted and the new one substituted.

Pastor John, though, had achieved even more here than the provision of some point of view. In fact, the point of view of a bureaucrat using a computer to delete references to "truth" and replace them with "knowledge" participated in the meaning of the example. The point of view (of controlling things through knowledge) shared in the meaning of the example story itself. Pastor John had his illustration as well as a nifty point of view. No more potential pitfalls in this sermon!

> *Hint:* For additional suggestions on the use of point of view, see chapter 5 of my *Narrative and Imagination.* There I suggest three models for point of view in preaching: the "camera model," based on Buttrick; the "video camera model," which adds sound and mobility; and the "flight simulator," which adds kinesthetic experience to those of sight and sound.

### For further reading

Carter, Stephen. *The Culture of Disbelief: How American Law and Politics Trivialize Religious Devotion.* New York: Basic Books, 1993.

Eslinger, Richard. *Narrative and Imagination: Preaching the Worlds That Shape Us.* Minneapolis: Fortress Press, 1995.

## 4.10. The Purpose of Illustrations

With the advent of the liberal era, biblical texts were assessed with regard to (1) ideational or conceptual interests (asking what a text's "theme" or "main idea" is) and (2) their experiential payoff (expressed in the personal feelings or affections of the reader). From these seemingly disparate elements, modern preaching with its points and illustrations arose and soon came to be an unexamined orthodoxy. At once rationalistic and romantic, the stereotypical three points and a poem embodied liberalism's ideological roots both in the Age of Reason and in the romantic movement.

How effectively this orthodoxy has dominated the American religious scene is revealed by its acceptance across theological positions and denominational traditions. For example, the dual commitments to rationalism and romanticism can be detected as easily in evangelical as in social-action preaching, as readily in Reformed or Wesleyan sermons as in Catholic homilies. Preachers have approached the Scriptures looking for themes to preach and experiences to impart to the individual listeners. (It is important to recognize the individualism of the liberal project, especially as it played out in preaching, a characteristic well documented by Richard Lischer in his essay "Preaching as the Church's Language.")

As the "triumph of the therapeutic" manifested itself in church and culture, this traditional and dualistic approach of liberal hermeneutics began to break down. Of the two component poles, the "experiential/expressive" (Lindbeck's term) became more central, with the discursive and rationalistic now reduced to a satellite orbiting the new star. Analyzing this shift in the formal liberal hermeneutics, Lischer detects a corresponding shift in the role of sermon illustrations. Though meant to express aspects of experience illustrative of some sermon idea or other, illustrations often assume their own life, leaving far behind the point they were designed to illustrate. Vividness of feeling now supplants conceptual reference in the determination of anecdotal illustrations, often justified by a reference to storytelling. Lischer concludes that "the sermon becomes little more than a vehicle for free-floating inspirational experiences, which are at best tangentially related to a religious truth or a vivid detail in a Bible passage" ("Preaching as the Church's Language," p. 125). Operating out of an experiential/expressive approach to the faith, such illustrations no longer illustrate; we have thereby arrived at a serious pitfall in present preaching practice.

Preaching that offers more or less free-floating inspirational experiences, I would argue, cannot in fairness be considered biblical preaching. While the communication of images and stories out of the lived experience of the hearers will almost always convey an affective dimension, faithful preaching must not be reduced solely to those experiences. The key is the notion of analogy. *An illustration (story, image, or example) must be provided as an analogy to the single meaning at stake within some portion of the sermon.* And we must evaluate that analogy *theologically,* with regard both to its effectiveness in depiction and to its appropriateness.

For example, in a sermon on the restoration of Zion in Isaiah 54:1-8, we might follow in sequence the scenes of the pericope as our homiletic plot. This would provide us with an initial exploration of the barrenness of Daughter Zion as she stands before God's promise of children, hearing the directive to "burst into song and shout" (v. 1b). The search for illustrations of this barrenness must

119

not be taken as license to inflict the congregation with experiences of social and existential barrenness. The image, example, or illustration is constrained by what is at stake theologically.

First, we note the covenantal context connoted by the image of the Daughter Zion. Second, any contemporary illustration is informed, if not constrained, by the dominant image system of barrenness as both the ruined city and its desolate women. (Katheryn Pfisterer Darr accurately notes that "Zion is both a city and the central female character in Isaiah's vision" [*Isaiah's Vision and the Family of God*, p. 178].) Third, our search for contemporary analogies to the text's image of barrenness will also be informed by the grace embodied in the proleptic announcement of deliverance. Our analogy, therefore, will be an illustration of barrenness within a churchly context, and it will be imaged with the dominant image system of the text in mind.

Within this section of the sermon, then, which of the following images of barrenness becomes most appropriate?

1. A news story of a mother using her welfare check for drugs rather than food for her child.
2. A first-person anecdote of a time in the preacher's life when the loss of his or her spouse led to considerable depression.
3. Reference to a recent issue of the denominational newspaper, in which the letters to the editor are anger-filled attacks of liberals against conservatives and vice versa.

The first illustration will be rejected, primarily because its analogy is to the contemporary cultural situation and not directly to that of the church. Here we spot a huge problem of preaching within the American church — the absence of any clear delineation between matters of God's covenant people and those of American society. If this illustration were to be used, it would be located elsewhere in the sermon, in a new single meaning where the social barrenness of the country is being explored.

A more profound issue at stake here, however, relates to a clash between the biblical image system and that of the contemporary illustration. In the former, the dynamic clearly involves a shift from metaphoric (Jerusalem as Daughter of Zion) and literally desolate women to a promise of new offspring in miraculous abundance. In the proposed illustration, however, the dynamic runs in the opposite direction — from a condition of motherhood to abandonment of a child. The grammar of the Isaiah image and the contemporary one would fight each other rather than function to establish a consciousness of analogy within the hearers. Most likely, the illustration would either delete from the congregational consciousness or, if retained, garble the opening section of the sermon and Isaiah's profound poetics.

Illustration 2 also needs to be immediately deleted from consideration, since such powerful first-person stories will most always blow away their conceptual context. (See Pitfall 4.4, "The 'I' of the Illustration.") The hearers will remember the preacher's story but will attach their own meanings and conclusions. "Maybe the pastor is depressed again and needs some more counseling." Notice that the first-person projection of feelings of depression from the pulpit will not necessarily evoke analogous feelings within the congregation. Responses may include pity, anger (at being manipulated), or perhaps just general discomfort.

The last of the three illustrations is the one we will select. It functions within an ecclesial context and effectively images barrenness. Point of view is also easily achievable — we could introduce the example by saying, *"Just this week, we received our (Methodist, Lutheran, etc.) newspaper. Turning to the 'Letters to the Editor' section, we read the epistles of anger, with liberals and conservatives hurling words like stones at each other, . . . each side blaming the other for all the problems in the churches."*

Some mention of the specific issue at stake in the most recent churchly culture wars also could be mentioned, although the preacher must tread cautiously here. The hearers could be lured into a focus on the issue itself (abortion, "family values," God-talk, etc.) rather than the impoverishment of the divisive church situation. Perhaps the preacher could continue by simply referring to the short list of issues, mentioning the most recent in passing. *"We all know the issues — sexuality, the family, biblical authority. Right now, we fight over an attempt to 're-imagine' God. The barrenness in Zion is clear, no matter which issue is hot and boiling over. We have lots of anger, and we dump it on each other in the name of everything that's good and holy.*

*There is barrenness in Zion. God's people are still tearing each other apart rather than singing out their praise as one."*

Recall the basic principle: within the lived experience of our listeners, we search for a concrete analogy to the single meaning at stake within each portion of the sermon.

### For further reading

Buttrick, David. *Homiletic: Moves and Structures,* pp. 127–58. Philadelphia: Fortress Press, 1987.

Darr, Katheryn Pfisterer. *Isaiah's Vision and the Family of God.* Louisville, Ky.: Westminster/John Knox Press, 1994.

Lischer, Richard. "Preaching as the Church's Language." In *Listening to the Word: Studies in Honor of Fred B. Craddock,* ed. Gail R. O'Day and Thomas G. Long, pp. 113–30. Nashville: Abingdon Press, 1993.

Long, Thomas G. *The Witness of Preaching,* pp. 156–80. Louisville, Ky.: Westminster/John Knox Press, 1989.

## 4.11. Going to the Movies

With the increasingly visual orientation of our culture, films — as well as TV plots — have become one of the richest sources for sermon images and illustrations. The icons and narratives of popular American culture may be rented at the local video store, checked out on cable, and seen at the Cinemax at the mall. Moreover, the generational cohorts within a congregation will most likely be self-defined in part by the characters, settings, and plots of a set of popular films. Trends in cultural change are often spotted first, or symbolized best, by the new movies being released. This constantly expanding resource continually informs and shapes the values, virtues, and character of church and society.

All of the above factors clearly argue for us preachers looking at films as a rich treasure-house of images and illustrations. As with any resource this powerful in its capacity to form and inform, however, the use of movies in preaching is not only filled with potential but

also cram-packed with pitfalls. Let's look at a few of the more prevalent pitfalls and the why and how of their destructiveness.

## The Personalities Agenda

Our culture's interest in movies goes far beyond an interest in the
narratives told on the silver screen. A glance at *People Magazine* and
an array of supermarket tabloids reveals the huge interest in the
lives of the stars. This reflects a cultural sickness, for people tend to
live vicariously through the "in" personalities of the day. In many
potential uses of film in preaching, we will find that unwanted and
unintended issues creep in regarding the actors and their own lives.
For example, in one preaching workshop, a sermon was preached
that used an illustration from the movie *Pretty Woman*. In the
discussion that followed, one listener commented, "I really don't
like Richard Gere"; another enthused, "That Julia Roberts is awesome!" The preacher clearly did not intend this kind of hearer
response from the illustration.

## The Generational Thing

Precisely because films do reflect the experiences of specific generations, we may find that a particular incident in a film is familiar to
us but not to members of other generational groups — and vice
versa. The preacher who is sensitive to such differences may therefore need to devote more attention to providing a context for a film
illustration than he or she feels is personally necessary. In other
cases, a particular film may present a context of meanings that speak
to the entire congregation.

## Cultural Myths of American Films

One recent area of investigation by biblical scholars has been the
mythic structures underlying certain modern films. An important
result of these inquiries for preachers has been the discovery of a series

of narratives that highlight and endorse several enduring myths of American culture. To invoke almost any reference to the Dirty Harry series, for example, is to invoke as well the myth of the solo savior, according to parables scholar Brandon Scott. (See his "Towards a Hermeneutic of the Solo Savior: Dirty Harry and Romans 5–8.")

While the savior-myth identified by Scott in the Dirty Harry series may be an unwelcome and unintended companion to any sermon illustration from the series, in other cases the preacher may well be homiletically attracted to a film precisely because of its positive mythic structure. For example, the theme of the desperate fight between good and evil, with its Jungian categories shaping the warfare, might be found to be excellent material for certain sermons, such as one based on the Johannine prologue with its motif of light versus darkness. If, for example, we cited an incident from a Star Wars movie in support of such a theme, we would also have to contend with the entire mythic structure of the Star Wars trilogy. Best described as pop Buddhism, this mythic worldview differs sharply from Christian notions of Incarnation, community-in-Spirit, discipleship, and eternal life.

Such complications should not lead us to avoid illustrations from contemporary films, for the characters and issues experienced at the local cinema or at home through a video are powerful shapers of individual and social imagination. The walls of our personal and communal consciousness are papered with these images. As we have seen, however, there are pitfalls related to our tapping of this awesome resource on behalf of preaching the Gospel. Much more inquiry is needed at this intersection of films and homiletics.

### For further reading

Scott, Bernard Brandon. *Hollywood Dreams and Biblical Stories*. Minneapolis: Fortress Press, 1994.

Scott, Bernard Brandon. "Towards a Hermeneutic of the Solo Savior: Dirty Harry and Romans 5–8." In *Intersections: Post-Critical Studies in Preaching,* ed. Richard Eslinger, pp. 123–56. Grand Rapids: Wm. B. Eerdmans Publishing Co., 1994.

# 5. Context and Delivery

The context for preaching is primarily that of a local congregation gathered for worship on the Lord's Day. From this perspective, the sermon is one act of worship, organically related to other acts of worship. Proceeding from the reading and hearing of Scripture and finding its responses in prayer, offering, and Eucharist, the sermon is a liturgical action. It springs from other words and leans toward the action of breaking bread at the Lord's Table.

Seen in this perspective, it is understandable that the renewal of preaching has trailed behind the reforms of worship by about a decade. With shifts in the liturgical context earlier in this century — specifically, once the Word of God was opened more lavishly to the people in both Roman Catholic and Protestant churches — the impetus was present for preaching to change as well. For the context of worship to be in reform also means that the qualities that stand for leadership in worship and preaching are also open to revision.

An important part of preaching is "delivery," by which we really are speaking of much more than voice and inflection. Rather, we mean by it the entire embodiment of the act of preaching in the stance and gestures, the intonations and rhetoric of the preacher. There has been a reconsideration of the old "pulpit prince" kind of oratory, along with a reconsideration of the role of the congregation. Now we see more clearly the essentially dialogic nature of Christian preaching. Yet there is one constant — in the midst of the people gathered for prayer and praise, Scripture is read and a servant of that Word begins to preach.

125

## 5.1. Isolationists

For most of the course of Christian tradition, the sermon was situated in Sunday worship as the event most immediately following the reading of the Scripture lessons. Equally persistent was the location of a sequence of events immediately following the sermon that were responsive in character (i.e., creed, prayers of the people, and offertory). The sequence was (1) the Word, read and proclaimed, and then (2) responses to the Word. The sermon was an organic portion of this sweep of Word and response, and even when preaching became obscured in the medieval church, there was no question where the homily belonged when it was restored by the Second Vatican Council.

Within some of the American Protestant churches, however, a glaring displacement of the sermon took place during the early decades of the last century. Under the influence of revivalism and with an antisacramental orientation, the sermon became dislocated from its place adjacent to the reading of Scripture and was placed at the end of the service of worship. Increasingly the sermon was regarded as the concluding brilliant gem of the order of worship, with all the other acts of worship now regarded only as the preliminaries. In many cases, the offertory stood as a sort of liturgical Grand Canyon that separated these "opening exercises" from the sublime sermonic summit. We can sketch this altered order of Sunday worship as in the figure below.

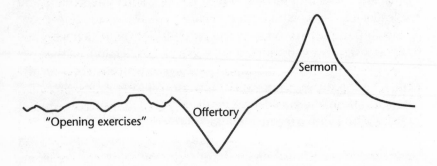

"Opening exercises"    Offertory    Sermon

The pitfalls related to this sermon-last liturgical innovation include several problems that have persisted in many churches until as recently as last Sunday. First, the severance of the close proximity between biblical text and sermon provides a liturgical justification for topical preaching. Little necessary relationship is evident between a text or texts (but usually only one) read as part of the "preliminaries" and the grand finale of the sermon itself. This pattern of worship provides the occasion for biblical minimalism in Christian worship to reach its nadir — a Sunday service of worship in which the only Scripture read and heard is the preacher's text prior to the sermon. Often this text consists of only one scriptural verse, which somehow is construed as adequate for the needs of the preacher and, presumably, the people.

A correlate to this biblical minimalism is that acts of worship that historically have served as the responses of the people now respond to nothing in particular. Dropped into the hodgepodge of the service's "opening exercises," the Psalms, for example, if used at all, become deadly dull responsive readings responding to

---

*Project:* Look at the Scripture lessons for the Sundays after Epiphany in Year C of the ecumenical lectionary. Each Sunday's Gospel lesson celebrates yet another manifestation of Christ's glory, and thereby invites a specific response from the congregation. For example, the theme of the First Sunday after Epiphany calls for the response of baptism or the congregation's renewal of their baptismal covenant. Similarly, the Cana lesson for the Second Sunday after Epiphany invites the liturgical response of the renewal of marriage vows. Now look at the following Sundays after Epiphany. What distinctive liturgical response of faith might follow the sermon given the intent of these lessons?

not much of anything. Other acts of worship that are inherently responsive to proclamation in the tradition, such as the creed and the intercessions, have also been moved to arbitrary locations where no such natural responses are invited. In contrast, the perennial response to the sermon now has become the altar call or the invitation to join the church. Interestingly, the same stereo-typed response has occurred, no matter what direction the preaching itself took, although the presence of that invitation has certainly shaped the goal of countless sermons over the past century and a half. As Charles Rice has observed, this invitation took the place of the Eucharistic invitation to the Lord's Table and consequently served to set preaching and the sacrament in opposition to each other.

### For further reading

Eslinger, Richard L. "Church Year and Preaching," in *Concise Encyclopedia of Preaching*, ed. William H. Willimon and Richard Lischer, pp. 74–78. Louisville: Westminster John Knox Press, 1995.

Rice, Charles L. *The Embodied Word: Preaching as Art and Liturgy*. Minneapolis: Fortress Press, 1991.

White, James F. *Introduction to Christian Worship*. Rev. ed. Nashville: Abingdon Press, 1990.

## 5.2. No Meals on This Flight

*Eucharist is not a ritual following the sermon from which one may or may not excuse oneself, but the community's meal with the risen Lord.*

Richard Lischer, "Preaching
as the Church's Language"

Luke's wondrous Easter story of the Emmaus Road (24:13-35) is at once a witness to the appearance of the risen Lord on that first Lord's Day and a chronicle of Lord's Day worship in the New

128

Testament church. The two aspects of the narrative dance together as Cleopas and his companion are met and questioned by the stranger. They are instructed as to Scripture's witness to the necessity of the Messiah's passion and death, and only then "his entering into his glory." At the climax of the story, they extend good Jewish hospitality, the stranger becomes host, and he is recognized in the breaking of the bread. Suddenly despair is transformed into Easter joy. So the early Christians gather together for worship on the first day of the week, gather on that day of Christ's appearances, especially at their common meals. And when the church gathers on that Day, just as on the Emmaus road, there is on the one hand a hospitality extended to the Word, to Scripture, and to proclamation and on the other hospitality now received at the Table of the Lord.

From the perspective of New Testament observance of the Lord's Day, the tendency in Western Christianity of making Word and Table an either-or proposition is both theologically aberrant and pastorally deficient. Pitfalls abound in church tradition and practice where it is assumed that the meaning of Sunday worship is completed within the scope of a service only of the Word (that is, a preaching service) or only of the Lord's Supper (as was the case in much of Roman Catholic practice before Vatican II). In the contemporary American church scene, the former is by far our greater problem. To tell the truth, a significant number of American Christians lack any expectation that their Sunday worship has much, if anything, to do with the Lord's Supper. When that service does take place, it is viewed as the exception; a service of non-Communion is the norm. The pitfalls of this practice are easy to catalog: individualism, a view of preaching as a personality-based feat, and a spirituality detached from the earthly ground of real bread and real life. The Sunday service of these American Christians might as well have a note printed in their order of worship: "No meals served on this flight."

A useful pathway toward the recovery of the complete Sunday service of Word and Table is suggested by homiletician Charles Rice, who speaks of "the end of the sermon." He trades on the double meaning of the word "end" — as both a boundary and a goal. Rice lists three senses in which the Lord's Supper, the Eucharist, is the end of preaching.

First, the aim of the homily is to bring people to make Eucharist, to speak of our life together in the light of Scripture in a way that leads the congregation towards thanksgiving and enables that to happen. The sermon is one movement in the liturgical action of the community, and in every case the aim of that movement is great thanksgiving. Second, the sermon is defined, its limits are set, by the Eucharist, by the essential Gospel that is embodied there. The person who preaches with the table in view may not preach on just anything or without regard for style appropriate to this setting. . . . Third, the homily is completed in the Eucharist . . . as members of the community gather around the table in anamnesis of Jesus, to lift up their hearts in praise and thanks to God. (*The Embodied Word,* pp. 18–19)

Rice's articulation of the Holy Meal as the limit and aim of preaching may in fact be heard as a commentary on Luke's narrative of the Emmaus Road. We gather around the Word on the way to break bread with our risen Lord.

When the Lord's Supper is viewed as the end of preaching — whether or not the Meal is celebrated every Sunday — preaching is actually liberated from several particular burdens. The preacher does not have to "say it all" on each homiletic occasion. He or she has a confidence that the sweep of the Gospel will be recited, sung, and enacted when the worship is completed at the Table. Moreover, the preacher is liberated from any shortage of ways in which to image the Gospel in the sermon. With the sermon "tending toward" its end in the Eucharist, a lavish table of imagery is now available by which to speak of grace, community, and the paschal mystery. Finally, there is a liberation regarding the person, role, and identity of the preacher. The one who preaches the Word (in most church traditions) is also the one who presides at the Holy Meal. To be known only as the preacher is to have the fullness of representative, ordained ministry impoverished, not enriched. But to serve as one who preaches the Word on the way to Emmaus and who presides at the Table of the risen Lord — that is a privilege of awesome mystery and joy.

*For further reading*

Rice, Charles L. *The Embodied Word: Preaching as Art and Liturgy*, pp. 15–91. Minneapolis: Fortress Press, 1991.

Saliers, Don E. *Worship as Theology: Foretaste of Glory Divine*. Nashville: Abingdon Press, 1994.

Sloyan, Gerald S. *Worshipful Preaching*, pp. 7–17. Philadelphia: Fortress Press, 1984.

Stookey, Lawrence Hull. *Eucharist: Christ's Feast with the Church*. Nashville: Abingdon Press, 1993.

Watkins, Keith. *The Feast of Joy: The Lord's Supper in Free Churches*. Saint Louis, Mo.: Bethany Press, 1977.

Willimon, William. *Sunday Dinner*. Nashville: Upper Room Press, 1988.

## 5.3. Pulpit Performers

> *Not only does the sermon-in-performance make a "self" and a "world," it also unmakes them. The sermon is a "site" for performance where the preacher may enter a free space created for serious play and unmask established orders and structures.*
>
> Richard F. Ward, "Performance Turns
> in Homiletics: Wrong Way or Right On?"

The pitfall of the "pulpit performer" is a serious one that probably all churchgoers have experienced, plus it is one that outsiders are quick to notice. Although it is serious, we nevertheless must be quite careful and precise in describing it. In a previous era of modern homiletics, "performance" was the pejorative label attached to a pulpit style that (1) imitated a famed pulpit personality or (2) copied a style shared by a certain school of preaching. It was quickly noticed, for example, when a preacher adopted a Billy Graham "evangelistic style" or a Robert Schuller "up with people" style. The pitfall in these cases relates to the suppression of a

131

preacher's own style and personality in favor of a delivery and rhetoric of imitation.

More recently, a number of homileticians have broadened the attack on "performance" in the pulpit by calling attention to the *persona* a preacher adopts, which projects a larger-than-life personality. The stereotype here is of someone "running for bishop" in certain church traditions (or we could substitute "running for moderator," "running for a big-steeple pastorate," etc.). Here, the projective style of personality is larger than life and may come packaged with practiced facial expressions and even a hairstyle tinted to match his or her pulpit outfit. Such a preacher is easily labeled a performer, which most commentators would view as a distinctly unfavorable description. Drawing attention to one's pulpit persona is at the opposite pole from the description of the preacher as a "servant of the Word."

The need for care and precision in this analysis of performer pitfalls in preaching arises particularly because of the more recent insight that any real-life act of preaching within Christian worship is embodied, dramatic, and a highly imaginative achievement involving both preacher and congregation. That is, Christian preaching is inevitably a performance in the truest sense of the word. Richard F. Ward is helpful at this point by locating the derivation of the word "performance" in the Old French *par-fournir*, which means "to furnish" or "to carry through to completion." He adds that "performing" literally means "form coming through" ("Performance Turns in Homiletics," p. 3). In this construal of the word, every act of preaching within the church's liturgy involves performance: rhetorically, the preacher's voice and body are necessarily involved in the event, and theologically, the preacher and people are necessarily enacting a highly imaginative event as the sermon is preached. In my *Narrative and Imagination,* I observe that "the liturgical event of preaching occurs never in a vacuum but within 'horizons of assent' of shared expectations and commonly held experiences" (p. 130).

Homiletic performance will be shaped by shared expectations of preacher and hearers, the location of the sermon within the order of service and within the liturgical space, its relative length, the role of vestments, and the use of Scripture. There is a "poetics of preaching" in which the performers (both preacher and hearers) are revealed to each other, even as the event of preaching most centrally is about revealing the Word.

One aspect of this complex performance that differs considerably from the "performer syndrome" is the question of self-consciousness. The pulpit performer appears highly self-conscious, managing every aspect of delivery, dress, and rhetoric moves with the goal of evoking a desired response from the audience. In fact, such self-consciousness is a primary symptom of one of preaching's most serious pitfalls. The bottom line here is hypocrisy!

For those gifted and called to preach, however, there is a refreshing self-forgetfulness during the event of preaching that parallels that of performers in certain sports and arts. Here the homiletic performance becomes a play in which the actors are themselves "played" by the enactment. Tragically, the self-conscious pulpit performer remains innocent of one of the greatest joys of Christian preaching — to forget oneself and be played by the Word.

### For further reading

Eslinger, Richard. *Narrative and Imagination: Preaching the Worlds That Shape Us,* esp. chap. 4. Minneapolis: Fortress Press, 1995.

Troeger, Thomas H. *Imagining a Sermon.* Nashville: Abingdon Press, 1990.

Ward, Richard F. "Performance Turns in Homiletics: Wrong Way or Right On?" *Journal of Communication and Religion* 17, no. 1 (March 1994): 1–11.

## 5.4. Space Invaders

Recently, at a clergy workshop that was not on preaching, a discussion on clergy roles in parish ministry was proceeding along. One colleague in the audience offered his opinion that he was strongly opposed to the "high and lifted up" view of the ordained, adding that as a way of showing his egalitarianism, he often preached "from in the midst of the people, up and down the aisle." The workshop leader, a pastoral counselor, immediately shocked the speaker and many others in the room by responding to this comment with an angry critique of such tactics and their rationale. The young clergyman was quite confused and hurt. Clearly he had stepped on a land mine (or fell into one of our pitfalls). But what exactly was the problem with doing something that seemed so well intentioned?

By way of responding to the colleague's reaction, it is necessary to back up a bit and analyze preaching as a highly complex event of imagination. I refer here to the aspects of the performance of preaching that are imaginatively held social constructs. For example, worshipers in our churches hold largely subconscious assumptions whereby they agree to (1) remain mostly in their respective seats and (2) give attention to the speaker, with such assumptions involving a skein of traditions, symbolizations, and theological beliefs. We may speak of this skein of roles and assumptions as an imaginative dance between preacher and people. This dance involves norms regarding, among other things, the spatial location for preaching in the context of the liturgy. In other words, the preacher and people hold a shared imaginative world in common that broadly defines the space for the people to assemble and the space for the preacher to provide liturgical leadership and preach. There will usually be rather well-defined locations for the hearers to hear (referred to as the nave, or simply the pews) and for the preacher to preach (alternately called pulpit, lectern, or ambo). These locations are highly symbolic and are the product of centuries of tradition.

Along with the embedded theological implications of this tradition, the spatial aspects of homiletic imagination also provide a sense of stability and security for the congregation. When the preacher respects these spatial assumptions and arrangements, it gives him or her freedom to challenge the congregation on behalf of the Word of God, speaking disruptive as well as comforting words to the hearers. Respecting the boundaries of the shared spatial map paradoxically allows more freedom for both the preacher and the people. Moreover, it is important to observe that this imaginative social mapping may range in its boundaries from congregation to congregation and from occasion to occasion. (For example, the acceptable boundary of the "preaching area" may be greater for a children's sermon, for certain holidays, or for worship services other than on Sunday morning.)

Even with all the exceptions, a readily identifiable "space" usually obtains for the preacher and the congregation.

The reason for the workshop leader's rebuke may now be more clearly understood. A major violation in the tacit norms as to the space of preaching — as in striding up and down the aisle — disrupts a congregation's necessary sense of security and emotional safety. With a growing sense of threat and anxiety, the listeners will typically extend less openness to the preacher's message, not more! Regarding the question of imaginatively held roles, pastoral counselor Keith Hackett is right when he states, "You cannot give away your role as a pastor and priest, even by walking up and down the aisles" (clergy workshop, Des Moines, Washington, March 1991). Here, in this "space invader" pitfall, we see the other extreme from that of the pulpit performer. Ironically, though, the space invader also calls more attention to him- or herself, all in the name of avoiding precisely such attention!

Some readers may object that the spatial limitations for the preacher have been set too narrowly. In response, I would point out that the space for preaching is usually elastic enough to allow modest forays outside the pulpit. Preachers have discovered that they can occasionally even preach from some other location in the chancel, including from behind the Communion table. Such adjustments fall within the scope of "the preacher's place" in most congregations. They do not, however, overlap the usual parameters of "the congregation's place."

Others may point out that during a dramatic sermon (for example, with the preacher adopting an "I, Zacchaeus" or "I, Mary Magdalene" persona), the acceptable range of the preacher's movement is considerably expanded, perhaps even including the church aisles in its scope. Such an exception, however, does not change the analysis here concerning the pitfall of "space invader" preaching. By virtue of the preacher's adopting the medium of drama rather than preaching, both preacher and congregation understand that a quite different skein of imaginative mapping now obtains; shifts in imaginative space between the two media (theater and the liturgy) signal shifts as well in the imaginative construal of the entire event. By the preacher's becoming a "character," biblical or otherwise, the hearers are still accorded their safety and distance, not as much through spatial distance as through the distance created by the characterization. What the preacher gives away in that shift to actor, however, is almost all of the possibilities implicit in the interchanges of the homiletic imagination during the performance of preaching.

### For further reading

Eslinger, Richard. *Narrative and Imagination: Preaching the Worlds That Shape Us,* esp. chap. 4. Minneapolis: Fortress Press, 1995.

## 5.5. The Bijou Blues

Imagine that you are a visitor to a large neo-Gothic church with high vaulted arches and a long center aisle. Dark wood and stained glass form the visual environment, along with the white marble of a "high altar." At the time for the sermon, the preacher mounts an even higher pulpit. Then, just before the sermon begins, a dramatic pause occurs involving a series of lighting changes. The house lights are dimmed while several spotlights on the pulpit are "dimmed up." In theater lighting terminology, a "cross-fade" has just occurred during the service of worship. If there was any question about the people's role before this lighting change, it is now quite clear that the assembly of the faithful have become a passive audience, sitting in semidarkness and awaiting the "performance" of the sermon. The pitfall is that of the Bijou blues; the people of God have been turned into a theater audience, and the preacher into a performer on stage.

Several mistaken notions contribute to this pitfall of the Bijou blues. We may consider the problems separately as they affect both congregation and preacher.

### Worshipers as Spectators

Although the worshipers are "auditors" (hearers) during the sermon, they are not truly an "audience." As auditors, they experience an ongoing dynamic of communication and relationship between themselves and the preacher. Whether with verbal cues such as "Amen" or "Preach it" or through facial expression and body language, the congregation is in dialogue with the preacher. By dimming the lighting in the nave, the people "recede into dusky spectatorship" (Charles Rice, *The Embodied Word,* p. 42). Little or no interaction is possible; instead, the people are told via the strongest possible cultural cues, "Keep quiet and watch the performance!"

## Worshipers as Individualistic

The dramatically dimmed sanctuary and the highlighted pulpit also serve to reinforce the propensity toward individualism among the hearers. Although almost every scriptural text is addressed to a community and to communal consciousness, the self-understanding of American Christians is predominantly shaped by a pervasive individualism, which represents an enormous challenge for the American preacher. To do this "dramatic lighting thing" within the worship of almost any congregation within our culture is to disregard this challenge outright and instead to subtly enhance an individualistic hermeneutic. The communal context of biblical faith will have a difficult time being communicated in the "dusky spectatorship" of a dimmed sanctuary.

## The Preacher as Romantic Performer

The Bijou blues also affect the preacher — both the preaching itself and also his or her identity. With regard to preaching, the spotlighted pulpit and dimmed nave are giveaways that the predominant model of worship is that of romanticism. A romantic piety assumes that the outcome of almost any service of worship is an aesthetic experience by the worshiper (individualism again!). The elements of romantic worship, including the sermon, are to be "uplifting," "beautiful," and "inspiring." A hard prophetic word or the offense of the Cross is distinctly out of place here; more appropriate are discourses on "the still small voice" and the beauties of the Galilean hillsides.

The preacher's identity is also at stake in this romantic lighting move. The lighting cue marks a distinction between the minister as preacher and as liturgist and presider at the Table. It is as if the "preaching moment" isolates one identity of the pastor and disconnects that office from the related liturgical and sacramental functions. Just as the congregation cannot be construed apart from its liturgical identity and function without loss (such as happens when the people become mere auditors), so too the preacher cannot have his or her liturgical and homiletic roles disjoined without loss. There is an ongoing engagement between leader and people that characterizes vital Christian worship, including the liturgical act of proclaiming the Gospel. To transform that context into a performance with an audience is to give away one of the most essential elements in Christian preaching — the dialogic interplay between preacher and people.

### For further reading

Buttrick, David. *A Captive Voice: The Liberation of Preaching*, pp. 33–53. Louisville, Ky.: Westminster/John Knox Press, 1994.

Rice, Charles L. *The Embodied Word: Preaching as Art and Liturgy*, pp. 71–91. Minneapolis: Fortress Press, 1991.

## 5.6. For Men Only

Carol Norén has commented that a preacher's nonverbal communication may involve profound images of self-disclosure, an observation that applies to both women and men in the pulpit. In fact, as Norén indicates, some of the most predictable images women convey in preaching are to some extent reactions against the more stereotypical male images of authority-bearing and dominating styles of leadership.

For a man, conveying authority in the pulpit may involve a traditional "dress code" in many Protestant settings — the dark suit of a bank president or the somber dignity of the Genevan gown. Gestures convey that same notion of authority through a series of hand gestures emphasizing or locating the points of the sermon. The emphasis often occurs through a movement of the hand outward and upward, with index finger extended. Such a gesture connotes male physical power, with perhaps a hint of the sexual. The "locating" of points or sequences in a sermon typically involves a hand gesture with fingers out and moving down as if making a move in chess. This gesture suggests an attitude of superior male intellect. To both may be added an almost subliminal sense of flirtation between the preacher and women in the congregation. Actually, a range of gestures, stances, and vocal intonations cluster around these two poles of stereotyped male imagery: the image of sexual prowess and power and that of analytic precision, rationality, and control.

The initial issue for men called to preach is exactly the same as for women called to preach. Problems arise when there is a dissonance between the preacher's nonverbal communication and the proclaimed Word. For some members of the congregation, a fine sermon delivered on the meaning of Christian servanthood may be shouted down by the preacher's expensive double-breasted wool suit, matching tie and pocket handkerchief, and hand-stitched Italian loafers. In contrast, gestures of precision and control resonate well, for example, with the nuanced argument of Paul to the Corinthians about eating or not eating meat (1 Cor. 10:23–11:1). The same gestures, however, may not be nearly as appropriate when dealing with Paul's words on freedom in Christ. The pitfall here obtains equally for women and for men — a preacher's nonverbal communication can shout down the best sermon in the world.

To the extent that the stereotypical image of the male preacher is that of one who has authority, is analytic, and is in control, a feeling of insecurity afflicts many of us men as we preach. (After all, we really know, in the depths of our soul, that we do not measure up very well to these cultural images.) Some of us may try to hide our insecurity behind a projected facade of extroverted "game show host" (see Carol Norén, *The Woman in the Pulpit,* p. 87), or we may try to imitate some favorite preaching model. Others of us soldier along, perhaps not saying much about our nonverbal communication but nevertheless "speaking openly" of what's down inside us through our gestures and delivery. A voice pitched just a bit too high, a pace that's slightly too

139

fast, perhaps even the fabled white knuckles grasping the sides of the pulpit — all these clearly signal our insecurity.

Another clear signal of preachers and teachers who feel a need to have things under more control than they do is the "birdcage" hand gesture. This gesture involves fingertips spread and paired together with the head bent down as if in search of the now-contained canary. The gesture speaks its message tellingly: "Help! I'm not feeling very together up here."

One way of dealing with these nonverbal signs of anxiety and insecurity is to examine with some care the idealized image of a preacher against which we measure ourselves. Obviously, we will feel insecure if our image of a preacher is overly heroic and idealized as compared with our own gifts and abilities. The alternative, though, is not the postured security of the old masculine stereotypes; rather, it is a sense of our own presence, with our own gifts and graces, as well as flaws and inadequacies. Clay pots for such treasure — that's who we are!

The other strategy for dealing with the overfunctioning masculine images of homiletic authority and control is to react against that model in just as severe a way as do some women preachers. Some men thus deliberately try to strike an opposite pose, forgetting that definition by negation is ultimately never very helpful. For the men, there is always the danger of presenting ourselves as "just one of the guys," a jovial sort who hands back appropriate authority as he rejects an unduly authoritarian model of the preacher. (See "Space Invaders," section 5.4, for one popular manifestation of this overreaction.)

There is also the pitfall of attempting to resolve these quandaries by presenting oneself as a victim, even if only through nonverbal means. This stratagem is becoming more common as a way to react against the old authoritarian model of the male preacher and as a way to deflect any critique of oneself as a male in the contemporary church. It may also signal that in fact the preacher has been a victim of some kind of abuse in the past. What is out of order here, though, is an attempt to sanction a victim status as a viable stance within the community in Christ. We must never forget that the fundamental issue is that of the congruence between the Gospel and the embodiment of the Gospel in our preaching.

> *Hint:* Homileticians are divided on how they evaluate nonverbal communication in the pulpit. Some colleagues see these factors as having little effect when compared to the issues of sermonic rhetoric. That is, they would stress attention to the way our language functions almost exclusively over the ways in which nonverbal factors may communicate. Other homileticians, like Norén, believe that the nonverbal elements in preaching are potentially harmful enough to be worthy of our scrutiny. Unfortunately, these factors are not best identified and analyzed by simply reading about them in a book. One of the best contexts to deal with these issues is in continuing education workshops in which the leader is skilled in dealing with issues of delivery and the embodiment of preaching.

*For further reading*

Norén, Carol M. *The Woman in the Pulpit.* Nashville: Abingdon Press, 1991.

## 5.7. For Women Only

In most regards, women and men within North American culture share a common language of gestures, facial expressions, and bodily stances. We receive much the same information from both men and women about the sourness of a pickle (squinted up eyes, nose, and mouth), the "unbelievable" comment heard just now (eyes looking upward and rolled), or a pose of thoughtfulness (lower lip sucked in with eyes glancing at a distance). A great deal of our culture's nonverbal communication is gender inclusive; we receive essentially the same information about a situation whether the sender is male or female.

Differences, however, do exist between men's and women's nonverbal communication, a fact that is critical for the women and men who are called to preach. Such communication is perhaps the dominant means of conveying attitudes and information about our sexuality. Moreover, a particular, gender-based language of nonverbal communication is strongly coded within church and society. As with the elements in stereotyped masculine identity and preaching, so too with women, the primary issue is one of an affinity between the nonverbal communication and the preached word. The goal, then, "for women (and men) in the pulpit is to be intentional rather than accidental about congruity between verbal and nonverbal communication" (Carol Norén, *The Woman in the Pulpit,* p. 86).

For women preachers, there are two primary types of discrepancies between verbal and nonverbal messages — the preacher as daughter, and the preacher as mother. Both pitfalls involve the communication of a specific feminine identity by the preacher through her nonverbal gestures, including facial expression and stance. Both also imply a construal of the entire context of the relationship between preacher and congregation. In analyzing these patterns, we benefit greatly from the insights of Carol Norén.

## The Preacher as Daughter

It is almost inevitable that a congregation will project onto their younger woman pastor some elements of the role of daughter in the family system. The pitfall is not here in this projection. What may lead to difficulty, however, is the unconscious strategy among some women preachers to shift the prevailing model of their relationship with the congregation from one of peers to that of daughter. The tendency toward this strategy is strongest in situations where the preacher may feel insecure or where she may feel that her message may be difficult for the congregation to hear. It may also show up more frequently at the beginning of a sermon. The particulars of this "preacher as daughter" type of nonverbal communication, according to Norén, involve a tilt of the head, "frequently accompanied by more shallow breathing, scissor-crossing of the legs (a truly self-protective gesture) and a rising inflection at the end of sentences (for example, 'shall we pray?')" (*The Woman in the Pulpit,* p. 82).

Some members of the congregation — women as well as men — may interpret these gestures and stances as attempts at being salacious. They are not. Rather, these cues signal an attempt to shift the model of the preacher-congregation relationship to that of daughter-parents. Along with being oddly incongruous with almost any conceivable biblical sermon, the "preacher as daughter" move also invites a deeper level of intimacy than many in the congregation may wish to extend. "In the latter case, the wobbling head will evoke resistance and perhaps impatience with what is perceived as inappropriate cuteness" (*The Woman in the Pulpit,* p. 83)

## The Preacher as Mother

There is also a certain inevitability about the woman preacher being seen as mother, both in her social role and in her identity within a congregational family system. As surely as a clergyman will come to assume a paterfamilias identity within a normally functioning congregation, so a clergywoman will as a matter of course gain a materfamilias identity. In fact, both social roles within a relatively healthy church family are so natural that an attempt by the pastor to give away this identity in the congregation will result in severe disruption to the system. Among the main aspects of the pastoral role and function, a clergywoman will normally bring a maternal identity to the pulpit. (Robert L. Randall has articulated these dynamics in *The Eternal Triangle.* He notes that a male pastor will typically have a primary female counterpart within the congregation, while a clergywoman will often gain a male counterpart. In many cases, that alternate person will be the clergy's spouse.)

As opposed to the "preacher as daughter" adoptive style, the maternal is more intrinsic to the normal complex of a woman pastor's identity. The role becomes problematic, however, when it begins to overfunction in preaching, when the sermon is heard as "what mother wants you to do." Here as well, certain identifiable nonverbal means of communication serve to convey an overbearing maternal image. One easy way to spot these stereotypical gestures is to look at Sunday comics dealing with families. Scarcely a Sunday goes by when a mother is not portrayed as being angry with her

143

child. She is drawn as standing with legs somewhat spread, one or both hands on hips, and chin tucked in looking down. A free hand will be extended out and down, possibly with the index finger pointing at the misbehaving child.

Consider Carol Norén's comment: "A woman in a position of authority awakens listeners' preverbal relationship with their mother. When her voice and body language challenge rather than soothe, listeners feel like rebellious children" (*The Woman in the Pulpit,* p. 85). Once more, I return to the key dictum with regard to these socially formed pastoral roles and perceptions — as fully as possible, the nonverbal communication of the preacher must be in congruity with the spoken word of the sermon. A dissonance here will usually result in a serious undermining of the ability to hear the spoken word easily and accurately.

### For further reading

Norén, Carol M. *The Woman in the Pulpit.* Nashville: Abingdon Press, 1991.

Randall, Robert L. *The Eternal Triangle: Pastor, Spouse, and Congregation.* Minneapolis: Fortress Press, 1992.

# Postscript

O ne possible response to this collection of preaching's pitfalls is that the result feels too constrained, too delimiting. For some preachers, such constraints may be welcomed, but others may find them unduly burdensome. After all, why not just get up on Sunday and let the Spirit both guide the sermon and deal with any difficulties along the way? True, the Spirit-wind blows where it chooses, as Jesus told Nicodemus, but there are disciplines of the Spirit that become the very precondition to freedom. Preaching is like that — the disciplines and constraints with which we struggle are correlates of the Word that sets people free. There really are pitfalls in preaching, and our task is to search out and avoid these entrapments on behalf of the liberating Word of God.

Some of the disciplines of preaching in any age deal with the limitations and possibilities of a culture's language and social consciousness. Preaching will always have these constraints imposed by the rhetoric of the times — as seen most clearly in the early Christian rhetoric of the New Testament. In these days, however, the rhetorical situation is in flux and quite a few of the old rules no longer obtain. And yet there are rhetorical disciplines that we trespass at our peril and at our preaching's peril. For example, just now, in this postmodern context, a continual dependence on vast, conceptual references — history, experience, mankind (or "humankind") — will mean that our hearers will be unable to retain and form our pulpit speech. A disciplined language of preaching, then, will be attentive to this constraint and frequently image the con-

145

ceptual material out of the lived experience of the hearers. In matters like the rhetorical environment of preaching, we cannot argue that the state of affairs should not be this way — it just is. We might well keep a lookout for further shifts in our culture's communal speech, but for now these rhetorical pitfalls are real and merciless. On the other hand, preachers with some rhetorical savvy may wield incredible freedom and creativity just now in the proclamation of the Gospel. It's just that this freedom comes along with the disciplines.

Another context within which we observe this interplay of discipline and freedom in preaching is at the level of interpretation. And here, the nature of the constraints and disciplines varies from that of the rhetorical context. It is not so much that "you can't do that and have people able to hear you." Rather, the constraints derive more from the entire hermeneutical model itself. Take the matter of distilling main ideas from texts, especially parable texts, as a persistent pitfall in our preaching. Here, "you can do that if you want," but the rationalistic model of interpretation that sustained main idea quests is an Enlightenment approach whose time has come and gone. To persist in such quests as preachers is to act out of a theological paradigm of a prior era. It also deprives ourselves and our hearers of the recent models of interpretation that have recovered the narratives and metaphors of the text and returned them to the sermon. So the freedom here is a paradigm of interpretation that restores the tensive and evocative character of biblical texts such as the parables. The disciplines of the emerging model include among others this restraint — we cannot return to the reduction of a "slow-cooking" approach and yet serve up a nourished banquet of the narratives of our biblical tradition.

One other issue regarding the interplay of discipline and freedom in homiletics needs to be highlighted . . . that of the ethos and character of the preacher. The pitfalls here are not gathered into one section of the book, but inhabit almost every aspect of the ministry of proclamation. We did notice that several pitfalls related to illustration were really, at their core, issues of ethos and character for the preacher. Claiming a first-person privilege for some story we "borrowed" from elsewhere is a violation of the covenant in Christ between the preacher and the hearers. Even if we can "get away with it," we lose and the congregation loses. The discipline of truth-telling will undergird our practice of preaching or all will suffer loss. Freedom does not come by way of compromises with the truth, in preaching or anywhere else! Likewise, we spotted issues related to the ethos and character of the preacher within the arena of rhetoric — the language we choose does reveal us to our listeners — and within that of delivery. As we observed, men and women preachers may encounter different pitfalls by virtue of broadly held images of gender in church and society. Here, too, we discovered constraints and were met by disciplines — for example, in over-reacting to the old images of the "pulpit prince" with his projective personality and affect-ladened illustrations. But we are discovering that the corrective is not in trying to give away the appropriate role of leadership invested in us by the tradition and through the congregation. This investment, whatever else it may be, involves a highly complex act of social imagination by the assembly, and we only deconstruct it with great care and on behalf of the Word. Once more, it is in discovering the constraints and disciplines within the guild of preachers that we find genuine freedom to preach. And in opposition to a recent time of overreaction against the constraints of our role and identity as preachers, we are now at the threshold of a renewed inquiry into the question of the character and ethos of the preacher. And those pitfalls are just now beginning to be assessed. This much is certain, though. The constraints and disciplines related to our virtues as preachers will serve to build up the freedom of God's people to hear God's Word; they will build up and not tear down. They will guide us as light to our path.

# Index